THE
DAISY
SERIES

THE F.M. LUPTON PUBLISHING CO.

HOW WOMEN

MAY

EARN MONEY.

BY

EFFIE W. MERRIMAN.

ORIGINALLY PUBLISHED IN

New York

BY

THE F. M. LUPTON PUBLISHING COMPANY.

Contents

CONTENTS.

CONTENTS.

CONTENTS.

CONTENTS.

CONTENTS.

PREFACE.

There are thousands of women in our country who feel the need of earning money, but who do not know how to go about it. The process of evolution has come too soon for many of them, and, as a consequence, they are dazed and sadly in need of a helping hand. They are not unwilling to be self-supporting, and so it seems all the harder that they must do with-out the necessaries of life simply because they do not know which way to turn in the great field of labor, where all is strange to them, and where everybody is too busy with his own struggle for bread to even heed their presence. It is to them that this little book is dedicated. Women who think of entering one of the many fields of professional work now open to them have progressed too far to be in need of such assistance, and will find nothing here for them. Neither are the salaried positions touched upon. To have done so would have been to write a book too cumbersome for convenience, since women now serve as clerks or assistants in nearly every department of labor, and, as a rule, their positions can never be traced to the knowledge of the contents of such a book as this. When all the women who incline to professional life, and all who are destined to teach in our public schools, and all who will serve as clerks and assistants, are taken away from the throng of women who must earn money, many are still left to whom the situation looks very hopeless. It is hoped that they may see this little book, and that they will find it suggestive. It is not meant to be more than that. It would be impossible to give complete instructions for the beginning and conducting of all the enterprises herein mentioned, because different conditions often necessitate different methods. One can offer suggestions as to what may be done, but no one can tell so well as yourself just how you are to do it. One thing is certain: You cannot succeed in any line unless you put yourself into your work. Your first thought must never be, "Is this as good as I am paid for?" but, "Is it as good as I can make it?" You must begin with a determination to succeed, and to stick to whatever you undertake until you do succeed. You can only become master of the situation by beginning as a slave to it, but never a blind slave or a machine. You must think and plan and contrive, and everything else must be of secondary importance until you have the mastery, and then you can take a long breath, for all your invested energies will be like well-invested capital, the interest on which will help to make life easier.

HOW WOMEN MAY EARN MONEY.

SMALL FRUITS.

Even a little garden devoted to small fruits may be very remunerative, if rightly managed, and it is a work that is found exceedingly fascinating by a majority of the women who have undertaken it. Says one enthusiastic advocate of small fruit growing: "To transform heavy, black earth and insipid rain water into edible rubies with celestial perfume and ambrosia flavor is, indeed, an art that appeals to the entire race."

It is strange but true that, to people living in the country, small fruits are very like heaven—objects of universal desire, but very general neglect. This may be caused, in large measure, from the mistaken idea that fine small fruits are difficult to raise. It is also the result of the ignorance of those who believe that they are so easily raised that it is only necessary to put some plants into poor, hard ground and leave them to fight it out with the weeds.

But there are women who have engaged in fruit raising as a means of livelihood, and have found it profitable. Women who live upon farms may, even if they only have a few hours each day to devote to the work, make quite a nice little sum of money by the raising of small fruit, and they will nearly always find a profitable market among their neighbors. When the land has been enriched and ploughed there is no work connected with the raising of small fruits which a woman of ordinary health cannot do. But a comparatively small outlay is necessary to begin this business, and, unless the soil or climate is very much against one, it nearly always pays, the degree of profit depending chiefly upon the skill, judgment and industry of the worker.

It is best to begin in a small way and to learn by experience and observation how to grow small fruit profitably. Do not expect returns before the second or third year. If you expect a larger market than that afforded by your neighbors, your fruit farm must be located where there is quick and cheap access to a city. Still, this is not absolutely essential, for many women make their fruits pay them well by canning them, drying them, or otherwise preserving them for market.

Throughout the Northwest strawberries, red and black raspberries, currants and gooseberries may be grown successfully; these, with the exception of the black raspberries, require no winter protection. The quality of the soil, as well as the lay of the land, must be taken into consideration, and preference given to that class of small fruits to which your surroundings seem best adapted. A fruit-grower of long experience says that, as a rule, soil that is rich, soft and moist is adapted to nearly all of the small fruits, and that there are none of them which will not do better if afforded a little protection through the winter and spring months by mulch spread over the bed. He believes that, taking one year with another, the best results are obtained by setting out the plants in September or October. He selects only strong, vigorous plants, and uses water freely while setting them out. He seldom allows them to bear at all the following year, but picks off the blossoms as soon as they appear, that all of the strength may go into the plant for the next year's bearing.

In this, as in other lines of work, one must have the best literature to be found on the subject, or expensive and needless blunders will be made. For instance, it should be known that strawberries are of two general kinds — pistillates and staminates — and that they must be planted together, since they are required to fertilize each other. There are many strawberry beds which blossom profusely, yet fail to bear fruit because of the exclusive use of either pistillates or staminates.

Two good crops of strawberries are as many as can be expected from one bed; then well-rooted runners should be taken up to form a new bed. Those who do best in the culture of strawberries set out new beds every year.

Raspberries should produce their best yield the second season and continue bearing up to the sixth year, hence they do not need to be renewed so frequently. With proper care, regular removal of old wood and careful pruning, currants should bear fruit for an indefinite length of time. Gooseberries also bear many years, if the bushes are kept well pruned. They should not be cultivated after the third year, for the roots spread so that they are injured by any attempt at cultivation. Strawberries are said to do best on low ground that slopes gently toward the south, and is so located that moisture may be supplied frequently. Raspberries and currants do best on high ground. Gooseberries mildew on high ground, but thrive in a low, rich soil. They may be made to bear nicely in a clay soil. One should have both early and late varieties of every class of small fruit that can be grown in her locality, in order that when people have learned to look to her for their small fruits she may be able to supply every demand.

No statement as to probable profits can be made that would not be misleading, for the reason that, like everything else produced from the soil, the season, the market, the fall of rain, the composition and many other things have to be taken into account. It is quite safe, however, to say that, taking one year with another, there is sure to be a reasonable profit from the sale of small fruits. This is frequently supplemented by the sale of plants.

TRANSIENT HOUSEKEEPERS.

There are ladies who, in middle life, find themselves obliged to earn their own living. The majority have only the ordinary education of the home so far as the preparation for work is concerned, with no special training in any given line, and to them the bread and butter question is a very serious one indeed. It is surprising that more of them have not thought of advertising to do housekeeping for short periods of time. There are many women who would avail themselves of a needed rest and change if they knew of some thoroughly reliable person who could take charge of the home and children for a short time. Then there are times when there is a large amount of sewing to which a woman must give her attention, or there is company to be entertained, or sickness keeps her in her own room, and at such times she would be glad to be relieved of all anxiety concerning housekeeping duties. All these are opportunities for the transient housekeeper. In some cases these positions would mean the actual work of housekeeping; in other cases it means simply the care and oversight of the home. The work requires patience, for no two households are managed in just the same way, and the one who goes from home to home must be able to adapt herself to different surroundings and to keep herself above all forms of gossip. In every line of business it is expected that they who work for short periods of time shall receive a higher rate of compensation than they who have permanent positions. This must be kept in mind by the transient housekeeper, who will not fail to impress the fact upon those who seek her services. Again it is expected that any one who undertakes this work shall understand every branch of it thoroughly, and such knowledge is worth a higher price than that given to the ordinary domestic. The transient housekeeper should not only know her own value, but she should never allow herself to be underestimated in any way. She should have a dignity of her own. Until she has as many employers on her list as she can serve, she will need to advertise quite frequently; but it will not be a great while, if she is really competent, before she will be making dates a long way ahead. The transient housekeeper must have a room or some place which she may call home, where she can stay when out of work, where her letters may be sent, and where they who need her services may go in search of her.

BOARDERS

Everywhere one hears the complaint that there is no longer any money to be made keeping boarders, yet the fact remains that there are a great many women who are earning a living in that way. One cannot succeed unless she is a first-class housekeeper and has the knack of cooking very appetizing dishes out of materials not at all expensive. Before going into this work, one must carefully consider her surroundings and not attempt to take ladies and gentlemen of leisure if the furniture is better adapted to the working girl. It is not safe to take a large house and furnish it unless one has had sufficient experience to know exactly what she can do.

One very pleasant boarding house was almost entirely furnished with goods bought at a second-hand store at a cost of a little more than a hundred dollars, but the lady who did it not only knew exactly what she wanted, but she could not easily be deceived in values, and she understood how to make old furniture look almost as well as when it was new. She had good taste and good judgment, and she could tell at a glance whether the furniture in a room was arranged as effectively as possible, or how it might be changed for the better. She knew how to give a home-like air to her surroundings. The food she placed before her boarders cost much less than that which they had eaten in other boarding houses, but they liked it better, for they said it tasted "almost as if mother had cooked it." Nothing was slighted. She knew how to make the most of everything. She had a child-like joy in her own successes, and all her boarders — her family, she called them — were interested in what she did, and felt more at home with her in consequence. Her house was always full, and she was obliged to turn applicants away almost every day.

Another woman pays the rent for her family by renting a large house which she has furnished and then subletting the rooms. She makes enough to pay her own rent and bring a fair rate of interest on the money she invested in furniture.

If one lives near a large college or other institution of learning, it is usually an easy matter to fill one's house with students, but, as a rule, they pay less than other boarders, and unless one has a very motherly heart they are not as satisfactory. There are women, however, who could not be induced to take any other class of boarders.

In many respects there is less annoyance in keeping boarders who belong to the laboring class than any others. Their work gives them good appetites, and as long as they have enough they are not disposed to complain if all the delicacies the market affords are not set before them. They will not object to a room with two beds in it so long as the beds are comfortable and everything is clean. The good housekeeper who knows how to cook plain food so as to have it appetizing need not fear to undertake keeping this class of boarders.

There are women who earn a living boarding and caring for motherless children, or those whose mothers are obliged to work. This is not unpleasant work to the woman who loves children, although, like anything else, it becomes tiresome at times.

There are other women who are born nurses, who board invalids or convalescents, who are not sick enough to be in a hospital, yet not well enough to work. Such a boarding house should be located in a quiet part of the city, where the air is good and the surroundings are cheerful. The landlady must understand how to care for the sick, as well as how to cook for them. She must expect to wait upon her boarders, doing for them what they are unable to do for themselves, and, of course, she will charge them accordingly. They will expect to pay more than at an ordinary boarding house, since she enables them to dispense with a nurse.

Many women who have pleasant country homes earn their pin money by keeping summer boarders. One woman, living on a farm that ran down to the shores of a pretty lake, conceived the idea of having a number of picturesque log houses built between her own house and the lake shore; then she advertised that she was prepared to board working girls who needed a vacation for three dollars a week. Her log houses are filled from early spring until late in the fall, and one must always engage board a long time ahead. She makes money at it, even though her prices are low, for she is an expert gardener, has a fine hothouse that insures early vegetables, keeps cows, raises poultry and almost supplies her table from her little farm. Her girls enjoy good, genuine country living as long as they are with her, and always return to their work rested and invigorated.

Another woman who has learned how to make her farm pay does it by boarding school boys during summer vacations. She has the entire upper floor of the barn filled with cot beds, and no boy can be induced to sleep in the house so long as there is room in the barn for him. The farm is situated in the woods, and the boys run wild without causing their elders any great amount of worry, for there is really little that can harm them. They adore the jolly couple who care for them, and try to obey them. There are many parents who would be glad to have their sons so well cared for during the long vacations, and who would not object to paying for such accommodations. To get such boarders one must, of course, have good recommendations from reliable and well-known parties.

PRIVATE HOMES FOR THE INSANE.

There are women who own large, comfortable homes, but who have small incomes, who are caring for the mildly insane as a means of livelihood. No more benevolent means of money-making can be thought of than this. There are many persons condemned to an insane asylum who are really harmless and who might, perhaps, become entirely cured if placed under conditions where they could be properly cared for, yet where they would be happy, and would not be obliged to feel as if they were in a prison under constant guardianship. In many cases the relatives are abundantly able to pay for the privilege of such a home, but do not know where to look for it.

The ideal place for such work would be a large country house, with fine surroundings and well walled in. It should be near enough to the city to permit of regular visits from a physician, as well as from the friends of the patients. All of the domestics employed should be chosen for their fitness for the position — that is, they should have the qualities essential to a good nurse, as well as the ability to do the particular work for which they are employed. Cheap help should never be sought. The boarding mistress should charge enough to enable her to employ those fitted for the work.

One who has the right qualifications for this work and the proper surroundings will have little difficulty in finding patients. She should tell physicians in all the nearest cities what she is prepared to do, and should also visit the nearest asylums, that she may have a talk with the officials. Very often they have a patient who has been placed on the convalescent list, whom they would like to have sent to some such place for a time before discharging him as cured, in order to see how he behaves when out from under hospital restraint. They would not bear the expense themselves, but there are few instances where the friends or relatives of the patient could not be induced to do so, should they recommend it.

LANDSCAPE GARDENING.

One woman of fine taste and quick perception makes her spending money by laying out yards and lawns for those who can afford to pay for such services. She employs a strong laboring man, who goes with her to help carry out her ideas; sometimes she gives work to more than one man. Quite frequently she is not asked to superintend the work at all, but simply to plan it. In that case she draws a picture of the lawn as she thinks it should look, and beneath it she writes the name of every tree, shrub and flower she has employed, indicating each one in the drawing by means of figures. She has an enviable reputation for her artistic rookeries and summer houses, and often superintends the erection of them upon lawns already laid out. She charges according to the amount of work she is required to do. While looking over her books at the close of last year she divided what she had received by the number of hours given to the work, and found that she had been paid at the rate of five dollars for eight hours' work. It would be good pay if she could get as much of the work as she could do, but, although frequently sent for by the residents of neighboring towns, she earns but little more than her spending money as yet. Every year, however, Americans realize more fully the desirability of having more artistic grounds around their homes, and she thinks there is a fair prospect of her work increasing.

She has had no lessons except those learned from observation and the reading of works on landscape gardening. She has traveled quite extensively, and has made many sketches of handsome lawns. She has, besides, many photographs of private and public parks. She is gifted with the qualifications that are needed to make her successful in this line of work, but says there is nothing about it that another woman might not learn, provided she has a taste for it.

PAPER-HANGER'S ASSISTANT.

The work of paper-hanging is entirely too hard for the average woman, but as an assistant she can be of considerable use, and should be able to earn fair wages. One lady assists her husband, who is a paperhanger, and he says he would much rather have her than a man assistant. Not only is she much neater, but she is more dextrous. Her work consists of trimming the paper, cutting it into proper lengths, spreading the paste and handing the paper to the paperhanger. Of course this, like any other employment where care should be used, requires some training, for it is very easy to spoil a great many dollars' worth of paper where it is of an expensive quality.

A woman of good taste might build up a nice business for herself by sending out circulars just before the spring and fall cleaning season, announcing her willingness to act as adviser in the matter of selecting wall paper. There are many women who long to have their homes decorated in good taste, and yet do not know what kinds of wall paper they should select to harmonize with their carpets and furniture. They would be glad to have some one relieve them of this anxiety. The lady can charge a certain sum for advice, and then she can give prices at which she will agree to hang the paper — that is, she takes the contract to hang it and then she hires a reliable paperhanger to do the work, with her assistance. She must, of course, have unerring taste and judgment besides a knowledge of the latest styles in paper, with prices, the best places to buy and the most competent workmen, with the wages they can command. She must also know how to figure the amount of paper needed for a room of any size or shape. If she is so fortunate as to have a friend who deals in wall paper, she can, without doubt, serve an apprenticeship with him, more especially if she is willing to do so without pay. Once in a paper house, she must keep her eyes open for opportunities to extend her knowledge. They will not be lacking, and if she is only observing and ready to embrace every opportunity, she ought not to be a great while in fitting herself to take contracts. When she has once made a name for herself she can easily get new houses that are to be papered throughout, and then her business will begin to be of importance. As her advice will necessarily be asked in regard to the finishing of the woodwork in the different rooms, she must not neglect this part of her education.

LOANING PERIODICALS.

There is a woman who writes very good practical articles, but she has not succeeded in finding a cash market for many of them. She lives in a small town where there is no library, and where there are women — and men, too — who like to read, but who cannot afford to subscribe for many periodicals. One day it occurred to her to start a circulating library of periodicals such as she could earn by writing. She knew that she would run a risk of incurring the displeasure of that large class of persons who would rather borrow reading matter than be independent about it, but she decided that the sooner they were given to understand that they must pay for the privilege of reading her periodicals the better. She immediately had a few circular letters typewritten, saying that it cost her to get the periodicals, and that she should be very glad to loan them for a consideration. It was not long before she had patrons who had longed to read some of the good things continually coming to her house, but who hesitated about borrowing, and she found many editors of good periodicals who were glad to take her manuscripts in payment for subscriptions. She does not earn a great amount, but she takes in enough to pay a girl to help about the work, and leave her time for doing what she likes better.

POPCORN.

Ours is said to be a nation of popcorn eaters, and there must be considerable truth in the statement, for popcorn furnishes a great many people with their bread and butter.

At all public gatherings, at summer resorts, at skating rinks — wherever people gather for entertainment of a public nature — there you will find the popcorn vender. The business seems greatly overdone, yet every one who enters it seems to sell his popcorn.

A neatly dressed young woman, of lady-like appearance, sells almost as much as her invalid mother can prepare. They have rooms downtown, and she runs home for a fresh supply as soon as she has disposed of a basketful. Only enough to fill one market basket with the five-cent bags is popped at one time, so it usually reaches the customer fresh and hot. The cleanest corn and the nicest butter is used, and one who likes popcorn and buys once is sure to become a regular customer.

The mother also makes delicious popcorn balls and cracker-jack, and some of both are usually carried by the daughter in a smaller and daintier basket. While they sell well, there is not as good a market for them as for the freshly popped corn.

TIN MENDING.

A bright young girl, who calls herself the boy of the family, having always been handy with tools, is now earning pin money by going from house to house for the purpose of mending dishes of tin and granite ware. She carries an outfit with her in a handy little case, and as she makes her rounds regularly, housewives have learned to know when she may be expected, and their disabled tinware or granite wear is piled up waiting her arrival. She is expert, and is making her queer trade profitable.

HORSE-RADISH.

A certain woman invested fifteen dollars in horse-radish roots, a horse-radish grater, vinegar and bottles. During the first year, after her horse-radish became large enough to use, she sold enough to replace the fifteen dollars invested and leave her twice the number of bottles she had when she began. Next year she cleared twenty-five dollars and did all her own work. The third year she paid a girl from the money she received from the sale of horse-radish, and had twenty-five dollars left, yet she had rested more hours than she ever had before. Her trade is growing nicely, for every one who tries her horseradish likes it, and she expects to pay her kitchen help and have fifty dollars next year.

CANNING, PICKLING, ETC

A woman who has become known as an expert in canning fruit and making pickles, preserves and jellies, can usually find employment during the fruit season. One woman does all such work at home. Her customers pay for the fruit, sugar and cans and give her a certain price per quart for her work. They find that the most satisfactory way, and the woman has all she can do. Another woman puts up all kinds of fruit as it comes into the market and sells it when the weather is cold. She sells part of it through the Woman's Exchange, but much the larger part is sold directly to the housewife. She has a number of small bottles with large mouths into which she puts samples of her fruit before starting on her canvassing tour. These bottles are packed into a large basket, and when the lady at whose house she calls has tasted some of the samples she is almost sure to give her an order for something. The woman who puts up the fruit says she finds few housewives who have put up all kinds of fruit for themselves and, having such a variety, she is sure to sell something at almost every house. She has an order book in which every order is carefully written. While putting up her fruit, she kept a strict account of all expenditures. To this she added her labor and the probable cost of disposing of her fruit, so she knows before starting out just what she must charge for each article on her list.

In addition to her canned fruits, jellies and preserves she has all kinds of pickles and catsups, chili sauce and chow-chow. Since much of this may be made late in the season, she is usually busy from early spring until after the holidays. It is a treat to go into her store-room and cellar, and one can hardly leave without buying some of the good things that are packed from floor to ceiling.

She has a small garden in which she raises a little fruit and nearly all the vegetables used in her mixed pickles and other relishes. She has a genius for compounding fruits into sauces that puzzle and delight the taste. One winter she sold a hundred cans of sauce that everybody liked, and few could tell was simply rhubarb and oranges stewed together and canned. She makes fine jellies of two or three fruits, and fruit butter that is made of several kinds of fruit, and is much liked by her customers. Some of these mixtures have fancy names of her own invention, and she refuses to tell how she makes them, claiming that her recipes are part of her stock in trade.

KINDERGARTEN.

Few pleasanter occupations are to be found by the girl who is interested in children than that of conducting a kindergarten. There are few, too, which offer better inducements.

The interest in kindergartens is constantly becoming greater; the demand for them is increasing, and the number of girls who are prepared for the work is comparatively few.

All over the country people are awakening to the value of the kindergarten training for their children, and with this growth of popular favor there must be a corresponding growth in opportunities for the young girls who take up the work.

Any bright girl with a good, common-school education, a liking for children and good health is ready to begin a training for the kindergarten.

Many times the question is asked: "Can a girl prepare herself thoroughly for teaching a kindergarten without attending a training school?" To the many girls who are asking this question eagerly, and who see no way of attending such a school, it is hard to be obliged to answer, "No," and yet this is the only answer that can be honestly made.

She may read Froebel's works and the other works bearing upon this subject, and thus become to some extent familiar with the methods of these schools, but there is an indefinable "atmosphere" in a true kindergarten which is one of its most potent factors, and this comes only from association with other workers and a thorough assimilation of the kindergarten principles. Aside from this, most of the kindergarten literature would be unintelligible to the general reader. These works are taken up paragraph by paragraph and explained, studied and assimilated in the training schools.

A girl may read the kindergarten books that are written in popular style, study the gifts and occupation material, and then establish a "play school" which will be a pleasure to herself and the little people who attend, but it will not be a kindergarten. There are hundreds of just such schools in this country, and they are usually designated kindergartens, but they have no real claim to that title, and thus named are a means of making the kindergarten misunderstood.

For the girl who cannot go to training school and who wishes to establish a "play school" for little children, the best plan to pursue would be to study Miss Elizabeth Harrison's "A Study of Child Nature," and "Nursery Science," by Florence Hull Winterburne; also Elinor Smith's "Songs for Little Children" and Emilie Poulsson's "Finger Play Book." It would also be well to subscribe for some periodical devoted to kindergarten work. Do not understand me to say that the play school is not legitimate and, in many cases where a kindergarten is not to be had, desirable — so long as it does not bear a name to which it is not entitled. The books mentioned, with a supply of the gifts and occupation materials of the kindergarten, will enable a girl to open a school for children which will be both pleasant and acceptable. But the underlying principle which gives each game a meaning, and which makes of the gifts and occupations a symmetrical whole, of which each is a necessary and related part — this will all be lacking because it will not be understood. Another item which must not be overlooked is that when an opportunity presents itself for real work in a salaried position, the teacher of such a school will not be able to fill it. Often, however, such a school can be opened and kept up long enough to enable the teacher to earn sufficient money to attend a training school later on.

The next method of preparation for the girl who cannot attend a training school, and one which may be pursued if the right sort of teacher can be found, is to offer her services in an established kindergarten in return for the instruction received. Before doing this she must be sure that the teacher of the kindergarten has herself been well trained, and must have it understood that she is to be taught the theory out of school hours, as well as the practice in the school.

The success of this method will depend upon the teacher quite as much as upon the pupil, and, although it is seldom really satisfactory, it is the best and only substitute for the training school that can be had. Even then, unless it can be supplemented by a short course afterward, it seldom prepares a girl for the best positions, although it may enable her to open a kindergarten of her own.

A training-school course may be completed in one year — that is, in nine months. Usually one is required to pay about fifty dollars for tuition and fifteen dollars for the materials used. Of course, where one has to leave home to attend school, there is the additional expense of board.

The training school combines both theory and practice. The students observe the work in various kindergartens in the city during the morning from nine until twelve, and in the afternoon they are in the school. Here they study the theories and methods of the kindergartens, and are taught simple music, drawing and physical culture, as applied to the kindergarten. They make the various kinds of handwork taught, and study the use of the gifts, the games and the plays.

At the end of nine months the student, if at all bright and capable, is competent to take charge of a kindergarten, and is granted a certificate to that effect. A second year's study is often taken, sometimes in connection with teaching, but it is not absolutely necessary. The tuition for the second year is twenty-five dollars, with no additional expense for material.

The reason the matter of the training school is urged is because thorough work is needed in all lines of employment, and they who hope to compete successfully along any line should realize this. Those in charge of the training schools are constantly receiving requests for teachers to be sent here and elsewhere. "But we must have competent teachers," is the word that comes, "not parrot kindergartners."

It would hardly pay to open a kindergarten for less than twelve scholars. The first cost of establishing one for that number would be twenty dollars for gifts and occupation material, five dollars a dozen for chairs, and five dollars and fifty cents for a table. A copy of Emilie Poulsson's "Finger Play Book" and of Elinor Smith's "Songs for Little Children" will be found quite necessary. The question of rent and fuel must be of local determination. A table might be made at home, and the expense lessened to that extent. It should be six feet long, two feet and six inches wide and twenty inches high. The top must be very accurately marked off in one-inch squares for the use of the gifts. A discount of ten per cent. can usually be obtained if orders are accompanied by cash.

The average price charged per pupil is seventy-five cents per week. It varies from fifty cents to one dollar, according to location and to the circumstances of the parents for whose children it is established. The hours are from nine until twelve noon. Materials and books are to be had from any kindergarten supply house. There are training schools in nearly all the large cities to which one can go for further information or to apply for instructions.

MUSIC TEACHING.

In these days the ordinary music teacher has rather a hard time of it, for her name is legion. There is seldom much to be made in a field of work that is filled with workers who are only half fitted for it. The one who is well fitted, while she must suffer because of the presence of the others, will always have something to do.

One woman has proven that it is possible for a member of her sex who is a thorough musician to make money in a school for music, even when it is started in the neighborhood of an established conservatory of music, presided over by a man of fine reputation as a musician.

This woman began by soliciting pupils from house to house, agreeing to take them for considerably less than the usual rate, provided she could have a class of twelve beginners to teach all at once. She used the blackboard as well as the piano, and, having been a successful teacher in the primary school, she understood how to teach beginners by applying methods that had proven successful in other branches of learning. She was enthusiastic and knew how to make her pupils work. She had a long framework fitted with keys, and her pupils were kept practicing on this improvised keyboard, at the same time being encouraged to watch each other and report any wrong fingering.

It would take too long to describe the various methods adopted by this woman who dared be original. Suffice it to say that her pupils learned rapidly, that they enjoyed two hours a day they spent with her, and that other pupils were soon applying for membership in her school. She would not take private pupils, and applicants were always obliged to wait until a class could be formed. The teacher was enabled to make the price so low that her pupils could come to her every day at first. She did not want them to practice at home until they had taken at least a term, for she preferred to watch them closely, that they would be less likely to form bad habits, and she considered two hours a day sufficient length of time for beginners to give to their work. This enabled children to begin, even if there were no musical instrument at home, and that pleased many parents who did not wish to purchase a piano until they knew whether or not they had a child possessing enough musical ability to make it worth while. In this way she secured pupils that no other music teacher would have thought of taking. She clung steadily to two rules: First, she would only take beginners; second, she would not teach except in classes.

She soon had as many pupils as she could teach, and she proved that it paid to dare to go out of the beaten rut in teaching music as in anything else.

BAKERIES.

One always thinks of a baker in the masculine gender, yet it is hard to see why employment so very feminine in its nature should be given over to men. There is one woman who did not believe in such a division of work, and who decided to start a bakery of her own. She always used her initials only when signing her name to any document, and it was generally supposed that her father owned the bakery, and she helped manage it. When the truth of the matter began to leak out it was too late for people to predict failure, as they would undoubtedly have done had it been known at first. In speaking of it once the lady said: "Custom can kill an enterprise, or at least retard its growth, although the slaves of custom do not mean to work such dire results. Father was never successful in any undertaking, and I had always done what I set out to do, yet there had never been a woman baker in this part of the country, and for me to have made known my intentions would have set every one predicting failure. Human nature runs after the successful, and kicks the unsuccessful a little farther down the hill of adversity. I did not mean to have one more battle to fight in the beginning than was absolutely necessary, so I bowed to the unwritten laws of custom and let it be understood that a man was at the head of my bakery. Had people begun to prophesy failure every one would have tried to have the prophesy fulfilled by patronizing my rival at the other end of the city. As it is — well," with a sweep of the hand, indicating her tempting goods and neatly kept shop, "you can see that I do not lack patronage. I began by baking bread that was first class in every respect, and by having hot rolls at a certain hour every day. Of course I baked other things, but I advertised my bread and rolls, and gave my first attention to them, for in this day we must have a specialty to advertise. I superintended everything myself, and tried to have it all of the best, and that is the only secret of my success, so far as I know. There is no reason why other women can not run bakeries if they want to do it and are willing to work hard enough. Of course they ought to serve an apprenticeship that would make them acquainted with all the different branches of the work."

A man and his wife who are no longer young have established a "Home Bakery" in my city which pays them well. They have a reputation for making the finest toasted rusks and cream puffs to be obtained in the city, and they sell quantities of them. Of course they sell other things to the customers, who walk many blocks for toasted rusks and cream puffs.

There is hardly a town of ten thousand inhabitants in which at least one "home bakery" cannot be made to pay.

FLAVORING EXTRACTS.

The wife of a commercial traveler, finding herself alone a great deal, began to look about her for some employment that would fill the long days of her husband's absence. She soon saw that she could get nothing to do unless willing to work every day, and she knew her husband would raise decided objections to any such arrangement, for he was abundantly able to support her. If she found employment it must be at something where she could be her own mistress. She knew how to make very fine flavoring extracts and acceptable perfumes, and had often made them for gifts to friends. She knew that the profits on such articles are very large, and she enjoyed the work. She could not peddle, but she knew a woman who could and would be glad of the opportunity, and so she purchased enough supplies for a start and went to work. She worked only during her husband's absence, and for a year he did not have a suspicion of the little business that was steadily growing almost under his nose. She felt obliged to tell him then, because she wished to move into a house where she could do her work more conveniently.

She has a number of women traveling for her now, and their samples include extracts of all kinds, blueing, liquid shoe blacking and perfumes. She hopes to pay for a little home for her old father and mother without help from her husband, and without doubt she will succeed.

PROPRIETARY GOODS.

More than one woman has made a fortune in proprietary goods, but all who have done so have had more than an average amount of business ability.

A certain business woman, who is well known over all the United States as the manufacturer of a popular toilet article, was once a clerk in a dry goods house. She chanced to learn that certain ingredients would produce certain results, and began to experiment, with no other thought than to supply her own toilet table. She succeeded in making a really excellent article, and soon her friends asked her to make some for them. She did so, charging what she herself had usually paid for articles of a similar nature, and little by little her trade grew. Then, being worn out with clerking, she decided to try to increase her list of customers a little faster. She gave a nice name to her merchandise, bought a box of bottles, had some labels printed, and did a little advertising. She showed her business ability by her choice of periodicals in which to place her advertisements. She now keeps more than one printing press busy in getting out her circulars, and, although she is still a young woman, she is listed among our millionaires.

It would surprise one who has never given the matter much thought to read the chemist's reports of the various proprietary articles which have become famous. There are few which might not be made at home, or which are really more efficacious than would be a preparation put up from a formula taken from an ordinary doctor's book. They are more famous because some one with good business ability foresaw that he could make money by advertising them. One should have considerable money for advertising purposes, if he would have speedy results, but that a large amount of money is not necessary in order to succeed eventually is proven by the experience of the lady just mentioned. One must have a really meritorious article to begin with, and then if one has a genius for advertising, success is sure to result in due time.

KNITTING FACTORIES.

In this day of cheap, ready-made, knitted underwear it would not seem that a living could be made in a knitting factory opened in one room of a dwelling house, but there is such a factory in a Western city that seems to support quite a large family. There are two knitting machines kept almost constantly at work — one run by the woman who started the factory, the other by the invalid husband and the eldest daughter. They make all sorts of knitted underwear to order, taking careful measurements and sending home garments that fit much better than the ordinary custom-made underwear. Then one has a choice of yarn used, which is a source of satisfaction. While the garments wear better than those usually for sale, their price is no greater, and so the business grows quickly, considering the fact that there is no advertising done except by the pleased customer who tells her friends. Besides knitting new garments, these people repair old ones made by them by cutting out worn places and setting in new pieces— a proceeding that appeals to the ordinary housewife and tends to make her a customer for an indefinite length of time. Stockings, mittens, leggins and sweaters are also made to order in this factory, and silk thread is used instead of yarn whenever desired.

HARES.

The fact that there is a certain time in the year when nice hares bring a good price in the market ought to suggest a means of earning pin money to those looking for something that may be done at home. Women who have tried raising hares for market say they are more profitable than poultry, for they require less care and bring a better price. As is well known, they are prolific. Many people like the meat of our common wild rabbit, but it is not so good as that of the German hare, and the latter possesses another point in its favor, being nearly three times as large as its wild brother. When well grown they often weigh twelve pounds. They can be fed on cabbage, hay and turnips during those months when grass is not abundant enough for their needs. They bear confinement well, and may be kept on a village lot, but measures must be taken to keep them at home, for one's neighbors are apt to consider them a nuisance. One writer on this subject recommends sinking galvanized wire netting into the ground about six inches, allowing the upper part to form a fence around their park. She says it is a good plan to place their house in the center of this inclosure, that they may burrow under it, for it gives them needed exercise.

FLOWERS.

In all cities and most small towns there is a demand for flowers and an opportunity for women who are successful in raising them to make a fairly good income by the sale of plants and blossoms — yes, and seeds, too. A Minneapolis woman makes considerable money selling her flower seeds, for which she has gained quite a reputation, although she has done but little advertising. There are several women now engaged in making perfumes and face washes from flowers, and others who make a little pin money preparing rose leaves for head rests and rose jars.

One should not attempt to cultivate flowers for profit unless she is, generally speaking, successful in caring for them. There seems to be an indescribable but necessary qualification possessed by some women that others do not have. With such women flowers always grow without giving any trouble, while other women care for theirs most conscientiously and still lose them.

One woman carries flowers to the downtown offices, going to each one during the week. They are all pretty, old-fashioned flowers, simply arranged in little bouquets that she sells for five cents each. She carries them closely packed in a basket. Another woman, an invalid, is brought into town in the morning and deposited on a street corner, chair and all. She has great baskets of cut flowers with her, which she arranges into bouquets during the day and sells for five cents each.

These women depend entirely on little, old-fashioned flower gardens for their pin money. Still another woman earns money by caring for plants through the winter for women whose houses are too cold to allow of their being kept at home.

Other women spend most of their time raising houseplants for sale. One woman earns a great deal of money raising early plants to be used for bedding purposes and for window boxes. Another supplies flowers for cemetery vases, and still another gives the larger part of her time to the care of bulbous plants.

One can usually do well in a village or small town which is not considered large enough to support a greenhouse, especially if she provide for a brisk demand on Christmas and Easter, and always has something suitable for weddings and funerals.

While it is well to have a conservatory, one can make a start without one, more especially if there are a number of sunny windows in the house. Many prefer plants raised at home to those raised in the greenhouse, for they suffer less in changing, and so are considered more satisfactory in the long run. One may, therefore, build up a nice little business, even if there are greenhouses near by. In this, as in everything else, it is wisest to begin on a small scale.

PRIVATE SCHOOLS.

Teaching has long been one of the favorite employments of women, and it does not lose adherents as the years go by. We are not dealing in these pages with salaried positions, so in this article will simply mention private schools as a means of money making. There are private schools for girls and small boys scattered all over the country. The majority of them are run by women, and nearly all are self-supporting, while some are paying well. A woman who knows how to teach, who has considerable business ability and a few good references, can nearly always succeed in securing pupils.

Two sisters once agreed to coach three young girls during vacation on the studies in which they had failed to pass the required examination. They taught them so well that at the next examination they led their class in these studies and, by studying with the sisters during another vacation, were enabled to pass into a higher grade. From that time on the sisters were constantly besieged by parents who were willing to pay well to have their children taught in their home, and now they have one of the finest private boarding schools in the East.

A girl with a little income of her own and a natural love for teaching manages to live more comfortably than her income would allow her to by taking private pupils. She opens a private school at one of the most fashionable summer resorts every summer and at a popular winter resort during the cold weather. She visits parents in person, shows her references and explains her methods. Her pupils are only taught from nine to twelve each day, and they have no studies to take up out of school hours. She succeeds in making mothers see that it is better for the child to study a little, even though away from home, that it does not injure its health in the least, and that it will be a relief to all the adults to be free from the children's noise for a few hours each day. She does not try to get a very large class, for she has no intention of working herself into invalidism. She simply means to piece out her income in the pleasantest way at her command, and her work is really more of a pleasure than a task. Because she feels that way about it, she is enabled to make enthusiastic students of her pupils.

A girl who is thoroughly well qualified to teach the deaf has located in one of our Western cities, where she is making fifty dollars a month more than her expenses by taking private pupils in lip reading.

A lady who had fine educational advantages, as well as the advantages of travel, was left in destitute circumstances, and now earns her living by teaching other women how to pronounce foreign words that are frequently used here. She also tells them of the sights to be seen when they are about to travel, illustrating by means of photographs, and gives them information that enables them to not only get the most good from their journey, but to talk of it when they return without showing their ignorance in every sentence they utter, as so many do. Her lessons last an hour and a half, and cost five dollars each. If two or three, or even more, wish to form a class and divide the expense, they are at liberty to do so; she has many of the suddenly-made-rich who would, on no account, have it made known that they felt the need of such instruction. She employs the conversational method of teaching, principally, and requires her pupils to write from memory, when they return home, a sort of synopsis of what she has told them. At the next lesson she questions them on the previous one in a way that shows that she expects them to be earnest students. Their wealth does not cause her to hesitate for fear of giving offense when criticism is merited.

Conversational methods of teaching are becoming more and more popular, and classes are being formed everywhere for instruction in foreign languages, in history, in current topics and in literature. These classes are most frequently taught by men, but there is no reason why they should not be organized by properly qualified women and be made to pay. Indeed, two of the best private classes in history ever organized are taught by a Western woman, who manages to live on what she is thus enabled to earn. One class is taught in the evening, the other in the afternoon, and every year she is obliged to refuse pupils who wish to join, because her parlors are crowded to the utmost capacity.

A flourishing school of elocution in the West is managed entirely by a woman, and in the same city another woman organized a school of music and made it pay, notwithstanding the fact that a man had already entered the field and won a reputation that seemed would eclipse all lesser lights.

Of late years schools where housekeeping methods are taught are becoming popular and open up a fine field of labor for the woman who understands how to teach as well as how to keep house. In these schools a term usually consists of twenty-four lessons. Prospective housekeepers are taught in the morning and working girls in the evening.

A woman in the West earns her living by giving lessons to foreigners of the working class. She teaches in the evening exclusively, and charges each pupil ten cents a lesson. She teaches them how to speak English, as well as how to read and write. She gives little talks on the history of our country and on current topics, which serve to vary the monotony of the study hours. She also gives them instruction in our laws and customs, and fits them generally to become intelligent citizens. She has three different classes, each of which meet twice weekly, and she averages a dollar and a half an evening for her work. She certainly could not earn more in any other way and have her days for her home duties.

There is a woman who has a class which she instructs in music, literature and art — not to be workers, but to know how to appreciate and criticize the work of others. She is a woman of more than ordinary talent, being able to do all these things in an acceptable manner, and, above all, she is a critic of discrimination. She knows how to take a book, a picture or a piece of music apart, piece by piece, and point out every little beauty, every little defect, every instance where the worker lost sight of his ideal.

Books, pictures and music that have been studied with her are always afterward used by the pupil as objects of comparison, and have an added value that is worth more than the price paid for instruction, which, by the way, is far from being a small one.

One of the latest fads is to organize classes for the cultivation of the memory. The one who organizes the class has previously invented some method whereby this may be done successfully in his opinion, and since one must be decidedly original as well as a teacher, many classes are not likely to be started as a means of money making by very many.

There is a very general desire for more education at the present time, and any one who knows anything particularly well and understands how to impart his knowledge can find some one to learn of him if he only tries hard enough.

TRAVELER'S GUIDE.

A woman who does not like to work and who does like to travel set her wits to work to discover how she might earn her living by doing that which pleased her.

She made arrangements with the superintendents of different lines and with hotel keepers at the various places at which she wished to stop whereby they were to take care of a certain number of travelers at a certain price. She always included herself in the list, but when she divided the price to be paid by the number of travelers to be accommodated she did not include herself. Thus each contributed to her journey without realizing it, but in no other way were they required to pay for her services. She planned the route, acted as guide, which her many journeys abroad fitted her to do acceptably, and relieved the other travelers of all the petty annoyances.

On her first trip she took a great many photographs, which were afterward arranged for a stereopticon. She got a literary friend to help her write a descriptive talk of the trips; then, when she reached home she went around giving lectures with the stereopticon views. She made enough in this way to support herself until it was time to start on another trip with another party.

She has now taken five different parties into foreign lands. Her lectures serve to interest many people, and make it easier to induce prospective travelers to agree to go with her.

It requires an immense amount of energy to earn one's living in this way, besides unlimited tact and the greatest of faith in one's ability. It would not be wise for the ordinary woman to attempt it, but this may meet the eye of one who is fitted by nature for such a career and who has not yet realized it, and so it forms a part of this book.

REMODELING HATS.

A great many women are making a living by remodeling hats. They understand how to press them into new shapes, sew them over, bleach and color them, and during the millinery season they are kept busier than the average milliner. One must serve an apprenticeship at this work before attempting to open a shop. She must also know how to dye feathers and recurl them, how to clean laces and how to rejuvenate mussy velvets and ribbons. There are not so many of these establishments but room might be made for more, and the woman who is just fitted for such work need not hesitate to undertake it.

ARTIFICIAL FLOWERS.

There are more than three thousand persons in the United States who are engaged in the making of artificial flowers, a majority being women. And yet the work is not so overdone but there is a market for flowers that are exceptionally well made.

One girl who supplies a large proportion of the flowers used in a wholesale millinery establishment never learned the trade of any professional. She had a natural aptitude for the work, and taught herself by picking the French artificial flowers to pieces and putting them together again. Now she uses natural flowers for her models, and her work is sold for "genuine French flowers." She has exquisite taste and such deftness of touch that she can make many more flowers in a day than can the average girl. She never seems to have to try; her flowers simply grow under her fingers, and never have the "stiff" appearance that is characteristic of the flowers made by women who have to try the second time to get a leaf in place.

This girl does her work in her own rooms. Her flowers are packed in boxes supplied by the wholesale house and so nicely labeled in French that they have the appearance of having been directly shipped from France. Indeed, they may have been, but the flowers are made in New York.

STERILIZED MILK.

Cow's milk is quite generally considered the best substitute for mother's milk, yet the mortality of infants artificially nourished proves that it is far from being satisfactory. Medicinal qualities contained in the food given the cow are liable to reappear in the milk and trouble the little one; then, again, milk undergoes a chemical change within a few hours after it is drawn, when it becomes really unfit for the child. As it is usually drawn but twice daily, it must be given at least twice during the twenty-four hours, when it has ceased to be good food. This fact has led to much experimenting by scientific men, and their results have brought about a new dairy industry that bids fair to be of interest to women from a financial point of view.

There are few now who do not prefer milk that has been Pasteurized or sterilized as an article of diet for the bottle-fed baby, but it calls for great care and work, besides some knowledge of the results sought, and so the dairyman who advertises to furnish such milk, and who can give good references, is bound to have a patronage. It is work preeminently suited to women, and it is hoped that it will, in the near future, furnish employment to a great many of them. While it is desirable that the woman who starts out to sell sterilized milk should have cows of her own, yet it is not absolutely necessary. She can purchase milk from some one near by, sterilize it and sell it for enough more to make a fair profit, and so make money until she can purchase cows of her own.

Machinery can now be purchased by the use of which large quantities of milk can be sterilized with little labor, but of course it is not to be thought of until a good business has been worked up, for it is quite expensive.

THE WONDERFUL CUPBOARD.

In a little village not many miles from Minneapolis there lives a woman with a wonderful cupboard. That cupboard is known all over the village, and the first thought of the woman who finds herself in need of something is, "I wonder if it might not be found in Mrs. Greene's cupboard?"

Mrs. Greene began her very good little business by taking an agency for some excellent salve and herb tea, put up by a well-advertised firm. Then she added some fine face powder, a highly recommended toilet cream and a wash that would remove sunburn. She divided the contents of boxes and bottles into smaller portions for the benefit of those who did not have money enough for the larger amount, and by charging a little extra for time and trouble made quite a nice profit. She obtained some first-class recipes and put up remedies of her own, giving preference to those requiring considerable work, knowing that there were many women who would rather buy than make them.

After a time scraps of silk and ribbon were added to her trade, and as it was the time when crazy patchwork was the fad, she had many customers who wanted just a little of some particular color to make out a block. The scraps were bought of a house in the East, who made them up into bundles of different sizes and values. These led, naturally, to laying in a small stock of material for fancy work, and as she was always willing to sell in small quantities, even to half a yard of embroidery silk, she was soon patronized by many women who would not have become used to going to her for such things had they not wanted a little of something of which they did not care to have any left over.

Perfumes, writing material, thread, dress facings, etc., etc., have gradually been added to the stock in trade, until now the cupboard, although kept in the best of order, is full almost to overflowing. A nice little sum is thereby obtained, and, although her housework has changed in character because of the added work of waiting upon customers, Mrs. Greene feels that she is kept enough brighter and happier, by seeing so many more people than she would otherwise see, to more than make good the time taken from scrubbing floors and making pies.

She is only an ordinary woman, and what she has done may be done by any one who will study the wants of the community in which she lives. Her only method of advertising was to let her neighbors know that she had something to sell.

INTELLIGENCE OFFICE.

A woman who is daily occupied in her own home and who has an average amount of knowledge of accounts might open there an intelligence office for domestic help. There are already a large number of such offices, and in order to make hers successful she should make it distinctive by advertising it as an office only for girls with recommendations. That point should be emphasized, and the rules made relative to it should be lived up to with great strictness. If the woman managing the business were a first-class housekeeper and could so arrange it, she might have, in conjunction with this office, a training school for girls. If her house were large enough so that she could allow girls from the country, or girls in the city who have no homes, to board with her until a place could be found, she would then feel as if she were doing some real good in the world besides earning her bread and butter. Fair accommodations could be provided for these girls at reasonable rates, more especially if enough of them were allowed to work for their board to make hired help unnecessary. Such an intelligence office would not pay well just at first; you must expect it to grow slowly, but if you work for a name more than for money you will find that it will pay you in the long run. The office should be so kept that girls would take pride in being sent from it, and would consider themselves lowered if forced to seek positions at ordinary intelligence offices, and mistresses should learn by experience that the help you furnish is seldom unreliable.

PINEAPPLES.

A Northern woman whose physician had advised her to look for a home in the South, and who was dependent on her own resources, found a family in Florida who agreed to let her work for her board in their home while she was learning the ways of Southern people. This family raised pineapples for a living, and our Northern friend had not lived with them a great while before she decided that she, too, could make her living by raising pineapples. Her employer had for many years kept strict account of all his transactions, and when she asked him how much capital she would need for a beginning he replied:

"You'll need at least one acre of land. That, in a good locality, will cost about a hundred dollars. It will cost fifty more to get it ready for cultivation, thirty for slips and about thirteen and a half to get them set. They will not bear for two years, during which time you will have to pay about fifty dollars for fertilizing the plants and twenty-five for cultivating them. The total cost will be about two hundred and forty-four dollars. When they begin to bear it will cost about twenty dollars for crates, picking, packing and marketing. You ought to have one hundred and fifty crates, and they should bring you a dollar and a quarter per crate, net. Your acre will bear for five years without renewal, and, although as much must be spent each year in fertilizing, it will cost less for work after the first year."

The lady decided to make the investment, more especially as she could get an acre of ground near by, and was still at liberty to work for her board. She saved a little by doing a part of the work herself. She sold the slips from her pines, and they brought in a little that helped. Her friend had been conservative in his estimates, and she realized more than he had predicted. She bought another acre of land and set it out to slips taken from her own pines, and the following year she bought a third acre, which was also set to pines. She thus had her groves so arranged that they would not need resetting at the same time. She now owns ten acres, which is as much as she can superintend, and is laying a nice little sum aside for the proverbial rainy day. Of course this could not have been accomplished without hard work, but now she takes life easily, and she has been in the South only a little more than eleven years. She showed her good judgment at the very beginning by living in the South long enough to become acquainted before attempting anything instead of rushing in blindly, as Northerners are too apt to do.

NURSES' BUREAU.

A good employment for a woman in her own home is that of carrying on a nurses' bureau. This occupation would not serve to furnish a livelihood from the beginning, but with a small outlay of time and money it would help to increase the family income. The first step necessary would be to obtain the names and addresses of good nurses. You can get them from physicians, from hospitals, from city directories and from friends and acquaintances. Next get permission from these nurses to place their names upon your list, with the amount of wages they ask per week and tell them what commission you would expect for securing them positions. If they will not agree to pay this commission you will, of course, strike their names from your list. Each nurse is then to furnish you with her address and to keep you informed of all her engagements, so that you may know at any time whether she is engaged or free, and where she may be found. When your list is long enough for a fair beginning advertise in the papers, send notices to the doctors and the hospitals and wherever else it occurs to you that there may arise a demand for such services. Keep a standing advertisement in some good paper to the effect that competent nurses may be obtained through you at any time. You must have telephone connections at your own home so that you may be reached without a moment's loss of time. If your home is large enough, it will pay you to take a few nurses to board, so as always to have some near at hand, and nurses will also find it to their advantage to make your house their home. In case you do not own a home, but rent, it will be wise to rent a house large enough for this purpose.

PLAYHOUSE FOR CHILDREN.

A girl of sixteen wished to earn money for herself, and was not allowed to leave home for that purpose. Her parents had begun building quite a large house, but had not been able to finish the double parlors. The girl obtained permission to use these rooms, and then she let it be known among her friends and neighbors that, whenever they wished to go calling or to get rid of the care of their children for a short time, she would make it her business to care for them for a small remuneration. She found many mothers in well-to-do circumstances who preferred doing their own work to hiring help, and who were very glad to be relieved of the anxiety of attending to their housework and watching the babies at the same time, who were glad to become her patrons. Aside from caring for the children at a fixed rate per hour, she added materially to her income by staying with them at their homes during the evening when their parents wished to go away. It is only by some such means that a great many parents can enjoy an evening away from home together, and if they could know of some competent person whom they could hire to care for their children many would gladly pay the sum charged. To do this work successfully, one must have a real love for children and a genius for entertaining them. A girl who uses slang or dresses carelessly or does anything that may be looked upon as a bad example for children to follow should never undertake this work, for most mothers will be loath to patronize her. A girl who is ladylike and who has a good influence over children will not be long in building up a paying business.

LINEN LAUNDRIES.

There are many housekeepers who would rather pay to have their doilies, lunch cloths and similar pieces laundered than to do the work themselves. It is work which any woman who can wash and iron carefully and well can undertake, if she have time and strength. If she gives her whole attention to it, it is not such a source of worry and annoyance as it becomes when undertaken by the woman who has a thousand and one other things to consider. There are few housekeepers who like to trust such washing to the hands of the ordinary washwoman or domestic or to the laundry. Since many of these pieces of table linen are embroidered in colors, the first thing to learn is how to "set" these colors successfully by means which will not injure the fabric. Another important item is the best method for removing stains which are often found on fine table linen, and which must be carefully and thoroughly removed before washing. Then one must know how to iron so as to raise all the embroidery, making it appear rich and heavy, and without tearing the finer embroideries or the hemstitched pieces. Most housekeepers like the idea of sending their table linen where it is not in danger of being washed with other articles. This work is not as heavy as ordinary laundry work, but it requires a great deal more care, and commands a better price in consequence. One woman at least has been known to succeed with this sort of employment. She now superintends her laundry, which is by no means an insignificant one, and employs a forewoman and a large force of girls. She has added fine laces, curtains and tidies to the list of articles she launders, but nothing else is undertaken.

VEGETABLES.

If you are so situated as to be able to raise vegetables for market you have a means by which you may earn more or less money every summer, the amount, of course, depending upon the season as well as upon your market.

It is said by women who have tried it that much more money may be made by peddling the vegetables from house to house than by disposing of them to other dealers, and that this part of the work is really not so disagreeable as one is inclined to imagine. It is no more demeaning to sell vegetables directly to the customer than it is to trade them off to a merchant, and when you have built up a little trade you will find many among your customers whom it will be a pleasure to meet each week. Most housewives are glad of an opportunity to get vegetables right from the farmer's wagon, so you need not feel, when people buy of you, that they are conferring any greater favor upon you than you are upon them. As a rule, they who sell directly from the wagon get nearly, if not quite, as high a price for their wares as grocers ask, while if they sell to grocers, they cannot expect to get much more than half the amount. This is right, too, although many gardeners grumble about it; but they should remember that the grocer takes all the chances of the goods spoiling on his hands before he can dispose of them. If you want to get what you think your wares are worth peddle them yourself, and instead of taking goods in exchange take cash and then spend it for what you want. You will be much better satisfied with the result.

If you can manage to have good vegetables a little earlier and a little later in the season than other people do, you can sell them more quickly and at a better price.

One woman gardener always manages to have green peas in August, and her regular customers are greatly disappointed when one gets all the peas and another can purchase none. She also has fine green corn when it is impossible to get it at the grocery stores, and it must be fun for her to peddle it, because it goes so fast.

She always has her garden made ready in the fall, then during the winter a coating of manure is spread over it. This is removed as soon as the snow begins to melt in the spring, and when the top of the ground can be worked she begins to plant onions, peas, turnips, radishes, lettuce and such vegetables as stand light frosts. The turnips are planted especially for greens, for which she finds a ready market, as they are not only palatable, but extremely good for one's physical health in the spring.

Some of her vegetable seeds are sown in window boxes while the snow is deep on the ground. She has a number of hotbeds, but plants get a good start in these window boxes before a hotbed can be used to advantage, and she makes money early in the spring by selling nice, thrifty plants. She has several south windows in her house, and each has a number of these boxes arranged one over another like shelves. There is, besides, a large flower stand covered with pots, in which her growing vegetables are transplanted as necessary. They are not as ornamental as flowers would be, but she says they pay better, and she must earn her bread and butter.

The soil for these window boxes is prepared in the fall and stored in a large bin in one corner of the cellar, which she had built for that especial purpose. The soil in her hotbeds is also made ready in the fall, in so far as that is possible. Tin cans are used in transplanting to save expense, and the thumb pots are of heavy paper. She makes them herself. The paper is covered with a sort of sizing that makes it durable, and the pots, when made, are filled with dirt and placed close together in a long zinc pan that looks like a baking pan.

All of her plants are kept out of doors for at least a week before they are transplanted, in order that they may be properly toughened by exposure, and so she loses very few of them.

When she sets out her earliest tomatoes she piles manure from the barnyard about them, not allowing it to touch the plant, but building it up at a little distance all around it like a barricade. This tends to keep the plant warm. She also has two dozen frames with glass tops which she sets over them, and she has early tomatoes to sell when prices are high. She says she gets more money from the two dozen plants thus cared for than from the five dozen set out later in the season.

Another secret of her success lies in the care she gives her vegetables when getting them ready for market. Everything is clean and wholesome and tempting. She does not try to make a little good stuff sell a great deal that is poor. Whatever she has speaks for itself, and she does not try to persuade people to buy, knowing that if they want anything of the sort at all they will surely want hers.

SOFT SOAP MAKING.

There are women who earn quite a little pin money by making soft soap. Of course they live on farms and so get almost for nothing what would make the article too expensive if attempted by women living in towns. On butchering days they save a large amount of grease from the intestines of the hogs that is quite apt to be wasted on farms, yet which is excellent for soap-making purposes. They also have receptacles in which they place the grease obtained by boiling refuse scraps of meat, skin and bones and skimming the water when it has become cold enough to allow the grease to come to the top.

Hardwood ashes are best for soap-making, and so the woman who undertakes to make soap for sale should live where she can burn hardwood, at least during the winter months.

The implements necessary to the making of soft soap are neither many nor expensive. Make a square support about a foot high on one side and about two feet high on the other. Nail a floor to this; then fasten a hogshead to the floor. Put a layer of clean straw in the hogshead, then throw in the ashes as they accumulate, but be careful to have them clean. Some women think it does not matter whether they are clean or not, since they are only to be used for soap, but such women never make a first-class article. Have a tight-fitting cover on the hogshead, to keep out dirt, flying leaves, etc.

When the barrel is full of ashes that have been well packed with a mallet, dig a hole in the center and pour in a pailful of boiling soft water. Add more water as necessary. When the lye has run off put it in a kettle over a steady fire and add grease, which, like the ashes, must be very clean. An old rule is to add grease until the lye will not eat a feather. Boil the grease and lye until it is thoroughly mixed, then pour it into your barrel, and be sure to stir it every day for a week. When done it should be of a beautiful pale yellow, so thick that it will scarcely fall from an inverted bowl, yet smooth and jelly-like in consistency.

One woman who earns pin money by selling her soap brings it to her customers in gallon crocks, and always takes home the empty crocks when furnishing a new supply of soap. Her customers say, "It looks good enough to eat." She is as particular about making her soap as she is about her jelly, for she says it is as easily discolored. Her customers appreciate her cleanliness, and always prefer her soap, especially for washing anything that is used about cooking, to that of any manufacturer whose methods they do not know.

VISITING CHAMBERMAIDS

Two young girls who did not like to hire out by the week conceived the idea of taking contracts to do chamberwork at a certain price per week. They applied for work in the hotels and boarding houses near their homes, and soon had as many rooms on their list as they could care for properly. They had regular hours at which they appeared at each house, and as they worked together, they soon left everything in good order. They felt that they had to make a name for extra good work and then to keep it, and they never gave cause for complaint. Many of the mistresses of boarding houses said that the visiting chambermaids enabled them to get along with one less girl, and that the work was done more satisfactorily than it ever was dene before.

The girls always had the afternoons to themselves, except on occasional days, when they were obliged to do a little sweeping in some of their larger houses. They earned five dollars a week apiece. It was no more than they would have earned had they hired out by the week, where their board would have been thrown in, but they liked this way of working, because it enabled them to remain at home a larger part of the time.

CARD WRITING.

One frequently sees men sitting at a table on a street corner, and they nearly always have employment, provided they write nicely. This fact was observed by a young girl who had lost her position and could not expect to get work in the same line at least for several months. She had a pretty gypsy suit that she made to wear at a church entertainment, and, after obtaining permission to place her table near the door of one of the largest department stores, she bought a supply of cards, pens and ink, donned her gypsy suit and went to work. Her suit was exceedingly becoming, and served to attract attention. She was a fine penman, and had a happy knack for pen drawing that sometimes served to amuse the crowd that gathered around her. Then she conceived the idea of tying half a dozen cards containing these drawings into little booklets, the purchaser being allowed to make a choice of the drawings for his book. She then wrote his name on the cover card, and it was finished. She sold a number of these booklets, and, with the cards she wrote, was soon earning more than she had received in her own place of employment. She purchased cards by the quantity and sold them at retail prices, and she kept a fine assortment from which to choose.

It would be unsafe for many girls to attempt this method of money-making, for they would be liable to be talked to in an insulting manner by a certain class of men. But this girl had a fine dignity of her own, and even in the most difficult situations was quite capable of taking care of herself, and compelling the respect of every one who spoke to her.

HOT COOKIES

A woman who lived downtown and who made exceptionally fine cookies conceived the idea of baking them and selling them while hot. She knew that there are few who can resist the temptation of eating hot cookies, if made by one who understands the art, and who cannot be induced to use poor butter. She had several children who hurried to the offices with their baskets of hot cookies, well covered, to keep them hot, and they sold readily at prices charged in stores and bakeries. She found that they sold best between the hours of eleven in the morning and five at night. There was a large, high school building near by, and she found many customers there. While her children were going to school she made arrangements with a young lady who was out of work and who was glad to sell her cookies on commission.

NEWS STANDS.

Why is it that most of the news stands are owned by men, when there are few employments better suited to women? Is it not because women fail to avail themselves of their opportunities? News stands are fairly profitable, else men would have nothing to do with them.

A young woman whose father died leaving a mother and several brothers and sisters for her to support decided to open a news stand, since there was nothing else she could do better. In addition to her periodicals, she carries a fine line of stationery, and she is supporting her family comfortably. She had once helped a friend who had a news stand during the holiday rush, when stationery sells well, and the knowledge and experience gained during that month were all she had when she decided to begin business for herself, but she has independence of spirit, pluck, energy and a natural taste for business, and so she is succeeding.

HOLIDAY GIFTS.

Three girls who longed for a little money for a special purpose spent most of their spare time for a year in making all sorts of articles both useful and ornamental. Nothing was thrown away during the year that could possibly be made into something attractive.

Just before the holidays they rented a room for a month and proceeded to so arrange their goods as to show them off to the best advantage, and then they did a little advertising. They had dainty hemstitched handkerchiefs, pretty crocheted hoods, comfortable knitted slippers for bedroom wear, embroidered center-pieces, cushions of every size and shape conceivable, dolls made of corncobs and nice, comfortable dollies of rags — in fact, they had such a variety of articles and all so nicely made that any one who entered their room was sure to purchase a nice holiday gift for some friend before leaving.

The girls said that the material they used had all been purchased a little at a time, with money that would otherwise have been spent in some trifling manner, and they really had not missed it at all. Then they had utilized many bits of silk and lace that had been accumulating for years, and every walk or drive into the country had resulted in an addition to their store. Their little baskets of spruce gum sold at once, and so did their pillows made of pine and fir and their cushions filled with the cotton from the milkweed. They could have sold twice the number of rag dolls, and every pair of knitted slippers were taken almost immediately. They realized enough from their year's work to take the little trip they had planned, and they really had not spent so much of their time in doing fancy work as to have it commented upon by their acquaintances.

They were girls who were not allowed to go away from home to earn money, but they had found a way to earn a little without doing so.

It resulted in their taking several of their friends into partnership and hiring a girl who made corsets for a living to act as their saleswoman. She was obliged to have an office downtown any way, and was glad of this opportunity to help pay rent.

While the girls did not make a great deal, they were enabled to earn a little in a pleasant way and yet stay at home.

BEDDING.

The woman who can make nice bedding and who knows how to work to the greatest advantage has a means of making money that is not usually taken into consideration.

One who decides to undertake this work should advertise among friends and acquaintances that she is willing to make bedding to order, to renovate it or to sell from her stock on hand. If she has a little money for the purpose, she might also advertise in the home papers and request those who are preparing wedding outfits to call upon her. She should have a stock for display embracing quilts of different designs, comforters of different thicknesses and cotton mattresses to go beneath the lower sheet, besides entire outfits for babies' beds. When one from her stock is sold it should be replaced as soon as possible with something similar. She should haunt bargain counters and opening sales, and never purchase anything for her quilts unless she can get it at a bargain, and when once she is started in her business she will find it to her advantage to keep a supply of material on hand from which her customers may make a choice. She will find many who will prefer to buy from her stock of goods rather than go to stores to make their purchases. Of course she will sell at the regular price — not the bargain price at which she secured it. She will also arrange to buy cotton batting in large quantities, so as to get a discount on it, and thread and tying yarn must be purchased in the same way.

There are many women who possess nice quilts that require care in renovating, or those for which they have an affection, although they may not be at all valuable, and many times they would be glad to have them made clean and whole. It is not easy work to renovate comforters, but some do it much more easily than others, simply because they know how. The woman who hopes to earn money in this way without working herself to death must know how.

MITTENS.

There is a dear old grandmother who makes her pin money by selling mittens of her own manufacture. She knits them of silk and worsted and coarse, warm yarn. They are fancy and plain, large and small, in sombre black or in pretty colors that take the eye of the child. Some have dainty bows of ribbon on the wrist; others are large and thick, and covered with leather. One can get any sort of mitten he may fancy by applying to her, or he may get his old mittens repaired at a reasonable rate. The grandmother likes to do this work, which is really the only kind of work she can do now, and although she does not get very high pay for it, what she does get is all her own and adds greatly to her happiness.

PIANO TUNING.

Of late years it is being discovered that women are as well if not better fitted for tuning pianos than men, having more sensitive ears. In most places a charge of two dollars is made for tuning a piano. Many people make contracts by the year whereby they get their pianos tuned four times a year for six dollars. When a piano is used a great deal by students it needs repairing as often as four times a year, and when one multiplies the number of musical instruments in use in a city, even by two, he is apt to be startled by the magnitude of the sum of money paid the professional piano-tuner.

One who thinks of taking up this work must manage to serve an apprenticeship in a large music house, even if she is obliged to give her time, and then she must be on good terms with the tuner employed there. She must learn how to put all manner of instruments in tune. When she starts out for herself she will, most likely, be obliged to solicit work by going from house to house, but at least one girl has proven that a good living may be earned in that way.

HOMEKEEPER'S AGENCY.

Not many years ago a lady who had gone from her father's house straight to that of her husband was left a widow in comparatively destitute circumstances. She had passed her fortieth birthday and realized that it would be difficult to take up any of the branches of labor by which younger women were enabled to earn a livelihood; yet she must do something, and it must pertain to housekeeping, for that was the only branch of labor in which she had any practical knowledge. The thought that led to the "Homekeeper's Agency" came to her one day when a friend chanced to say that she wished she knew of a woman who could make and drape curtains. This lady did know of one, and believed she could be hired, although she had never sought such employment.

"How much will you give me if I get you a good, reliable woman who can do the work artistically?" she asked.

"Half a dollar," was the prompt reply.

"I'll undertake it," she said, with equal promptness.

That set her to thinking of the vast number of women there were like that woman whom she meant to try to engage, who could do some one thing beautifully, but did not know how to make their one ability help them financially.

"And there would be just as many who would be glad to pay for their help," she exclaimed, as her idea matured, "and I'll bring them together!"

She spent some time in looking up women who could do things well, then she had circulars printed, which she sent to the women who could afford to hire things done. They read as follows:

DO YOU WANT ASSISTANCE IN

Mending and washing laces?

Hanging your draperies?

Selecting furniture?

Arranging your rooms artistically?

Remodeling your gowns?

Doing your millinery at home?

Cleaning your upholstered furniture?

Covering your worn chairs?

Preparing for your reception?

Caring for your teething baby?

Writing your club essay?
Putting up your fruit?
Coaching your boy for examination?
Teaching your daughter social observances?
COMPETENT, LADY-LIKE HELP FURNISHED BY
THE DAY OR HOUR BY
THE HOMEKEEPER'S AGENCY.

It was some time before all the women to whom she had spoken were given steady employment, but persistence in advertising and in sending out the circulars and careful supervision of all work obtained had its effect in due time. Now a great many women are employed regularly, and many more stand ready to take the orders that cannot be undertaken by the regular force.

The regular help is paid by the week. They come to the agency — the home of the agent — in the morning and remain there during the day except when sent out on an order. Their pay goes on whether they work or not. When they work the agent receives the pay, which averages about fifty cents an hour on short jobs.

To succeed in this business one must know when the work to be undertaken is well done. She may not be able to do it well herself, but she must not be deceived as to the quantity or quality of work done by one of her employees in a given length of time. She must be able to direct other women and to inspire their confidence. She must be businesslike and thorough, and she must drop in upon her employees while at work often enough to make them feel that she may be expected at any time, and that carelessness on their part will not be overlooked.

This is a business that cannot be built up in a day, but there is a good field in every large city for the right kind of a woman.

SWINE RAISING.

A Nebraska woman has made quite a reputation for herself as a breeder of fine Poland China hogs. Her judgment is held in high esteem among men engaged in the business, and people come from long distances to her annual sales.

It only proves what many women do not yet realize — that many of the employments now monopolized by men offer good opportunities to women of pluck and energy.

The woman who lives on a farm may find a nice little competence in the raising of swine, if she only cares to undertake the work. She will be more sure of success if she begins with one or two hogs and works up as she earns money for finer buildings and finer breeds. Journals devoted to this line of industry are to be had, and much practical information may be obtained from the best agricultural papers.

One farmer's wife who has made an agreement with her husband whereby the hog-raising has become her part of the work, buys the feed used of her husband, and hires the hogs butchered and marketed; yet last year she cleared a hundred and fifty dollars, and she said she had given less time to the work than many women spend over their embroidery. She says she finds it easier to raise hogs and buy her embroidery of women who prefer ladylike employment to that which brings a good price, but is not one of the avocations usually pursued by women.

This woman takes orders for pork and lard among the working class in a neighboring city, agreeing to deliver the goods on a certain day at a certain price, and it pays her much better than to sell her hogs in the neighboring markets. She manages to have small pigs about the holiday season, which nearly always sell well, and she has a good demand for live hogs during the spring. She keeps a book account of all transactions, and knows, to a penny, how much she makes or loses. Of course there are years when she gets little for her work, but, taking one year with another, she says she makes more than she did when a girl teaching school and with less work and worry.

CARING FOR HOTEL CHILDREN.

An enterprising school teacher spends her vacations at a fashionable summer hotel in the mountains, and is criticized for her seeming extravagance by some of her acquaintances who are not in her confidence. She had stopped at that hotel for a day or two several years ago and had noticed how neglected were the children of those guests at the hotel who could not afford to bring governesses. So she resolved to return and offer to take charge of the children for a certain length of time each day for a small sum per hour. She amuses the children, takes them into the woods for little picnic dinners, guides them in their various amusements and keeps them entirely away from their elders during the time they are under her care. The children are delighted, and she has enough of them to care for to more than pay her expenses during her vacation.

PROFESSIONAL DUSTER.

Already a number of women, intent on moneymaking, have assumed this title, with all that it implies; but the field is not yet crowded.

The professional duster must be neat in attire and business-like in manner. She will carry a hand-satchel filled with a fine array of dusters, and she will have regular appointments at houses whose owners have a bric-a-brac that is too precious to be entrusted to the ordinary servant. She will dust everything carefully, put it in place, see that curtains and scarfs are gracefully draped, and when everything is in order will hurry away to fill her next appointment. The nature of the work makes it impossible for her to make many engagements, because most housekeepers want their sweeping done on Friday, and the dusting cannot be long delayed; but as she has a home of her own to care for, it is really as much as she cares to do, and it gives her a little pin money all her own.

STORY-TELLING.

A young lady who was not strong enough to do hard work conceived the idea of earning money by telling stories to children. She had a natural talent in that direction, and a little rehearsal each day soon brought back the natural training in elocution that she had had while at school.

She read stories and then repeated them in language that children could understand. Each evening she told one story of adventure, one of history and one based on ethical laws. Frequently this was followed by a fairy story, and, to send her audience home feeling as if they must come again, she often announced that it would be finished in the next evening. She got the teachers in the different schools to announce her intention to tell stories to children, and from the first she had a good audience. As she charged but five cents admission and only kept the children between the hours of eight and nine, parents allowed their little folks to attend frequently. She told stories three evenings in the week, and averaged two dollars per evening after paying for hall, lights and heat, and also for the services of the young lady who sold tickets of admission. It was not a large sum, but she could not have earned as much in any other way, and it really required but a small portion of her time.

ETIQUETTE AND DANCING.

A young lady who had been a leader in society was suddenly thrown upon her own resources for a livelihood and after a careful review of her accomplishments decided to earn her own living by means of those which had hitherto brought to her the praises of her acquaints. She sent out circulars announcing that she would start a class in dancing on a certain evening, and that classes in deportment would also be conducted. Her name was so well known that she had no difficulty in securing pupils, for many mothers who did not believe in dancing were glad of the opportunity to give their daughters the benefit of the instruction in social laws and customs from so competent a teacher.

She also gave private lessons and had many pupils whose wealth gave them a place in society, but whose early advantages had been meagre.

An acquaintance with this class of people led to another opportunity for making money— that of the supervision of the entertainments they gave. She would take entire charge for a specified sum per evening, which was willingly paid by women who wanted their entertainments to be in good style, and were not sure that they knew just how to make them so.

UNDERWEAR.

A lady and her daughter living in a busy Western city earn their bread and butter by making underwear for women and children and nightshirts for men and boys. A number of their acquaintances predicted they could not succeed because ready-made clothing could be made so cheaply at department stores, but they believed there were many ladies who loved dainty underwear, and were able to afford it, who would be glad to have theirs finished more neatly than any they could purchase ready made. They were right, as their increasing orders have proven. They thoroughly understand cutting and fitting, and take as much pains with the fit of the garments they make as they would if making a dress. They charge a good price for their work, but their customers are all from the wealthy class, who are able and willing to pay well for that which exactly suits them.

This enterprising mother and daughter now employ several assistants— one to make knitted lace, one who furnishes crochetted trimming in dainty patterns, a third who is noted for the beautiful buttonholes she makes, and a fourth who does fine embroidery. There are, besides, two girls who run the sewing machines, and one who does hand finishing. The mother and daughter take orders, wait upon customers and attend to the cutting and fitting. The work is done in their own home, and they are so busy that they have no time to grieve over the past, when they entertained handsomely in the parlors now devoted to their business.

POULTRY RAISING.

"If I were consulted as to the best work for a woman who has only part of her time to give to it — something which can be carried on successfully both in country and town — that will give the most pleasure and profit for the least expenditure and time, I should say, 'By all means, let her engage in poultry raising.' "

The above statement is quoted from one who has tried different methods of money making, and who finally became a successful poultry raiser.

When we consider that the United States does not produce nearly as many eggs as are consumed by its people, it will be readily seen that poultry raising as an industry is not overdone, and that it offers an opportunity for women who must support themselves. But a small outlay of money is actually necessary for a start, although, of course, with a little capital judiciously invested one may have larger profits and lighter work.

In making a start it is wise to purchase fowls in the autumn, when they are cheapest, and when any reliable dealer will sell you a good flock at comparatively small cost rather than take the chances of being forced to keep them through the winter. Twenty hens and two cocks will be found a good number with which to experiment. They are not too many to be kept in one shed, and may be as easily cared for as a much smaller number. The shed should have windows facing the south and east, and should be well ventilated and reasonably warm. It should be provided with roosts made of poles or boards not less than two inches in width, and, in addition to comfortable nests, there should be a box of dust and ashes for them to roll in and plenty of good, clover hay or unthreshed wheat straw in which they may be kept busy scratching. If you have not capital enough to provide a shed of this sort, better not go into the business at all until you have.

Before purchasing your stock you should decide whether you mean to have eggs or chickens for the market. Of course this must depend, in a large degree, upon your location. If you are near a good market you will probably find that broilers and young chickens will pay best. If a long distance away you will probably do best to sell eggs, provided you learn how to pack them so that they will keep fresh a long time. All fowls do not do equally well in any climate, and you would best select your first flock from one not many miles away from your own home that you know have done well. If you wish early chickens you will find the light Brahmas or the Plymouth Rocks quite satisfactory; if you wish to sell eggs the Wyandottes are unexcelled. You must, of course, subscribe for some good poultry journal, and after you have been in the business a short time you will begin to have ideas of your own on the subject, and will probably change your flock more than once before you are entirely satisfied.

Women are natural poultry raisers, being better economists than men, and when we remember that the profits of poultry raising depend on good judgment and close calculation in small things, it is easy to see why, as a rule, they succeed better than men.

One who follows the plan of selling the eggs and poultry just when money is scarce, or when he happens to be going to town, will never realize much from his work. It is better to wait for good prices, then send both chicks and eggs to market in such a way that they give evidence of the best care. One must work not only for the best present price, but for a reputation that will insure a good price at times when others get a small one.

It is not a good plan to depend simply on hens. Try raising ducks, geese and turkeys also, for often when the market is dull in one line it is good in another. In all cities there is now a market for down for filling cushions and comforters, and they who keep ducks and geese may add considerably to their profits by keeping the down separate from the feathers when dressing their birds for market. Some women make quite a little by saving nice tail feathers and pretty wings, which they sell for dusters and for millinery purposes. The plumage of the white goose readily takes dye of any color, and one may add greatly to the results of the year's work by saving it to sell to those who make feather trimming, or they may make it into feather trimming themselves. A gentleman once took a lady to task for wearing a bird on her hat, and was greatly astonished to learn that she had made the entire bird from the feathers of the white goose, and had, beside, manufactured a large case full that she had sold at a good profit to a milliner in an adjoining city. Another woman has made quite a sum of money making boas from the feathers of her poultry. So you see there are a number of ways in which one may make money from poultry, in addition to selling the eggs and chickens.

Even if one has capital enough to furnish a large poultry yard it is not wise to do so unless she has had some experience in the business. Better save her money until she is sure what she wants. In any case she should keep out of debt and avoid the purchase of high-priced incubators and such things until she has the experience which will enable her to make a wise selection.

There is no part of the work that is too heavy or hard for a woman to undertake, although there will be found many tasks that are not entirely agreeable.

CLEANING OFFICES.

More money is to be made cleaning stores and offices than by working out by the week, and although this is not one of the pleasantest of occupations, it yet furnishes food to a number of women with families to whom a portion of their time must be given. As a rule the work must be done in the evening or the early morning. In most of the larger buildings in cities, salaried janitors are kept by the proprietor for such work, so the applicant must seek her employment in smaller buildings, where, as a rule, each tenant provides for the cleaning of his own office. If the woman does her work well and at the usual rates she will keep it year after year, and many supplement the income thus obtained by other work to be done during the middle of the day.

HOP RAISING.

Quite recently the papers have been telling of two sisters who are making money raising hops. They do all of the work themselves except during the season when the hops are picked and packed for market. Then the work must be done so quickly that they are obliged to hire considerable help. They say that there is nothing about the work much harder than many of the tasks that fall to the housewife, and that it is all much pleasanter, and they advise girls who are longing for independence and are living in the States adapted to hop culture to consider this source of money-making before entering some salaried occupation, where they will be paid about half what is paid a man for the same amount of labor.

These girls took a worn-out farm that was sold under foreclosure of mortgage for about half its true value. They borrowed money to purchase the farm and pay the expenses of their start, and in five years they had paid every cent of what they borrowed besides all their living expenses in the meantime. They had both worked on farms where hops were raised before they decided to earn a livelihood in this way.

COTTAGE CHEESE.

Of late years many women earn a little money by the sale of cottage cheese. As a rule they sell it through grocery stores and women's exchanges. Some sell directly to restaurants. In all cases, when the third party comes in, the price paid the maker of the cheese is very low. It is better to peddle your wares from house to house and get the price the housekeeper usually pays the grocer. You can take orders as you go, and so have an idea as to where a part of your next lot of cheese may be disposed of.

One woman has worked up a trade that requires the milk from eight cows. She makes part of her cheese quite dry, works it into little cakes, wraps parafine paper around each one and sells it for five cents a cake. A larger part of it, however, is worked dry, then made soft with thick, sweet cream, seasoned for the table and packed into glass cans holding a pint. She has no difficulty in selling this at ten cents a pint, and she claims that it pays well. When asked to do so she leaves the can, calling for it next time, and she always calls at a house on a certain day of each week, so as to be expected. She has a different set of customers for each day in the week. Of course all do not buy every time, and what is left after supplying the regular customers is either put in a store for sale or used as samples in an attempt to get more customers.

ADVERTISING.

It is a reflection on the inventive faculty in women that nearly every good advertising scheme has been evolved from the masculine brain. This is an age of advertising, and every one who has merchandise or other commodity of which he is anxious to dispose is glad to be helped to a method of introducing it not yet done to death by some one else. A woman with inventive genius will do well to set to work along this line of endeavor, for there is money in it.

An increasing number of women are engaged in writing advertisements, a branch of literary work that has been found quite remunerative by those who have the ability to do it acceptably. Two sisters, living in the East, earn considerable pin money in this way. One writes the advertisement, and the other illustrates it, and they submit their work directly to the manufacturer. Of course it necessitates a knowledge of the manufacturers who advertise, but every periodical can give information on that subject to those who study the advertising columns. Not only should the person who thinks of attempting the work study the advertisements for addresses but in order that she may see what sort of work has already been accepted.

DOLL'S DRESSMAKERS.

One old lady who has a liking for dainty sewing earns quite a little spending money by making dolls' clothes for sale. All her friends and acquaintances send her the scraps of silk and wool and laces for which they have no further use, knowing that every little scrap has value in her eyes. But the demand for her doll clothing is so great that she is often obliged to purchase material, and so her friends are always looking for bargains for her especial benefit. She keeps quite a stock of her tiny outfits on hand — some hanging up, others packed carefully in boxes. Her customers consist of nearly every child in the neighborhood, besides fond parents, uncles and aunties who are looking for gifts for fortunate little girls.

No small part of her income is derived from the lessons she gives in cutting and making dolls' clothes.

She charges each little pupil ten cents an hour, and as she is very particular about having the work done nicely and has a natural gift for teaching little folks, there are many mothers who are glad to have their daughters take lessons of her. They know that later on such instruction will help them greatly in cutting and fitting their own dresses. She never allows a child to stay longer than an hour at a time. When a pupil becomes proficient in cutting, fitting and making dolls' dresses, she receives a cunning little diploma, painted by the dear old white-haired dolls' dressmaker, and every child thinks it worth working for.

PEDDLING NUTS.

A Minneapolis woman supports a sick husband and three small children by peddling nuts. The nuts are cracked in the evening, the husband being able to assist in this part of the work, and great care is taken to get the meats out whole. A long peach basket is prettily lined with paper and fitted with a pasteboard cover that is trimmed with tissue paper and looks very attractive. This basket contains the nuts, a pretty salt bottle full of salt and a small glass in which to measure the nuts. She sells them for five cents a glass, and usually makes a dollar and a quarter a day. Most of her customers are found in offices, and she calls at so many places that she seldom visits the same office oftener than once a week. She carries English walnuts, as a rule, but sometimes the basket is divided into compartments, and one can have a choice of three varieties. Sometimes there are pretty little bags containing squares of cocoanut. A ten-cent cocoanut is made to fill four of these bags and brings her twenty cents. Quite frequently there are little bags filled with peanut taffy, which she makes very nicely, and often the peanuts are simply candied over — sugared peanuts, she calls them.

She thinks this is a better way to support her family than to try to get washing to do, for now she has nearly half of her day in which to attend to her home duties.

INFANT'S OUTFITS.

A woman who is able to do fine sewing nicely may build up a fairly good business making infants' outfits. She will have to understand how to do dainty hemming, hemstitching, fancy applied stitching and plain embroidery. Hand work is now given the rightful preference over machine-made embroideries and laces in the wardrobes of the little folks, which adds to the opportunities of the woman who desires to make her living by furnishing infants' outfits. As a rule, it is wise for a woman who is skillful with her needle to develop some specialty, for advertising along this line will attract others much more readily than one for ordinary sewing. This is also true with the sign which is placed on the house. You may put out one with the words, "Fine Sewing" upon it, and it will scarcely be looked at, whereas one bearing the words, "Infants' Outfits" would immediately attract attention.

A woman who goes into this work should always have on hand several complete outfits, and there should be considerable difference in their value. There should be an outfit that would be likely to attract the wealthy woman, as well as that which can be afforded by a laborer's wife. In most cases orders will be given for outfits, for many mothers have ideas of their own which they wish carried out. There are cases, however, where the customer wishes to purchase at once, and whenever a part of an outfit or a complete outfit has been sold it should be replaced immediately, that it may be in readiness for new customers.

PARLOR MILLINERY.

Parlor millinery offers a fine opportunity for ladies living in towns, villages or thickly settled country places. To succeed in this work a woman must have taste, a good eye for color, some business ability and a fair knowledge of millinery. She should have an attractive parlor, and her chances of success will increase in proportion as she is a charming hostess. It requires but little cash to start in this business, and only a portion of one's time need be given it.

One enterprising lady who went into parlor millinery had her parlor furnished with comfortable lounging chairs and made a practice of serving tea and wafers to her guests. It was a good idea, for ladies like nothing better than to visit together under such circumstances, and their orders are always enough more elaborate to pay for the expense of the refreshments. At one side of the room was a cupboard with glass doors where trimmed hats and bonnets were kept, and there was another cupboard with glass doors in which was a fine display of ribbons, etc. There was, besides, a chiffonier in which were kept the bonnets whose owners did not wish them to be seen until they appeared at church.

A lady who has a home or any financial backing can obtain a full supply of millinery from wholesale houses without a cash payment. The terms are so arranged, as a rule, that the first payment shall be made in thirty days, another in sixty, etc., giving an opportunity to dispose of some of the goods before the first payment comes due. If the stock has been chosen judiciously, with due consideration of the taste and the length of the pocketbooks of the probable customers, there should be little loss. It is wise to make the first order a small one, for in these days a supplementary order can be filled and delivered very promptly.

In addition to the hat frames, laces, ribbons, etc., needed in millinery, there should be a small stock of neckwear and dainty toilet articles which all girls delight in, but which few country girls have an opportunity of choosing for themselves, for, as a rule, those of good taste and style are not seen in country stores.

The lady who embarks in parlor millinery should keep herself posted on all the latest styles, and she should insist on selling to her customers only that which she knows to be becoming and in good taste. She must not allow the customer to buy two yards of ribbon when one could be used to better advantage, for her best advertising will be done by the bonnets she sends out.

It is said by those who have tried it that one may make about fifty per cent. on the capital invested in this business, and that there is the double advantage of being able to attend to one's ordinary occupations while building it up. The stock should be purchased but a short time before the season opens, and as one is buying for one's friends and neighbors, a knowledge of their requirements should keep them from buying unsalable articles. A woman with common sense and good taste will meet with little loss even at first, and will find in parlor millinery a very pleasant way of earning a little money.

CITY GUIDES.

In large cities many women piece out their incomes by acting as guides to lady strangers who come with their husbands on business, and who would otherwise be obliged to remain at an hotel until the husband had leisure to accompany them on a sight-seeing expedition.

These guides usually get permission to place their cards in a conspicuous place in the bedrooms and on the parlor tables in hotels. The cards give their references and addresses and the price expected per hour. They have rooms near the center of the city, and can arrive quickly upon receiving a telephone message from the clerk. They sometimes fee the chambermaids who are instrumental in getting them employment, and are thus often called to the attention of a lady who would not otherwise think of employing them. They must, of course, know all of the direct routes to all parts of the city and how to get there with least expense. They must know how one may see the most that is worth seeing in the least time, and they must be able to read character well enough to form a fair idea as to what each visitor would consider best worth seeing.

JEWELERS.

There are two sisters in New York, both under thirty years of age, who conduct a jewelry business and make it pay. One is an expert clockmaker; the other repairs watches, and both understand how to mend jewelry and set stones. They are pleasant and chatty, and prefer to act as their own clerks whenever that is possible.

One who contemplates going into this work should apprentice herself to some good jeweler, where she can become proficient in every detail. It is impossible to say how long a time will be required to learn the trade, for much depends upon the ability of the apprentice, as well as upon his opportunities. One can often learn faster with a jeweler in a country store, where there is little help, and the apprentice has an opportunity to try her hand at everything. If she can supplement such training with a few months with a jeweler, she should then find herself thoroughly well fitted to open a shop for herself.

A girl who had learned how to repair clocks and watches and mend jewelry opened a little shop for herself less than three years ago in a busy Western city, and is gradually working into a nice business and accumulating a stock of which she has every reason to be proud. When she began she had only her tools, and was obliged to rent table room in a department store. She has paid her own expenses and kept out of debt. She is a good workman, doing well what she undertakes, but, of course, she cannot do as many things as the experienced city jeweler. She has earned for herself the reputation of knowing how to repair a watch or clock and of not sending it home as bad as when she took it, as too many jewelers do. Every one who has gone to her for such work is sure to recommend her to some one else, and that is always the best sort of an advertisement.

SHOPPING.

To be able to make a business of shopping for others, one must possess good taste and good judgment. With these two requisites and a little money for advertising purposes, to send out circulars, etc., a woman who lives in a large city may be able to build up quite a business in this line. Recently a few enterprising shopping agents have sent out drummers into the neighboring country towns who take samples of dress goods, table linens, etc., and take orders which the shopping agent fills promptly. One important item which tends to insure patronage is the fact that no commission is usually charged those for whom the shopping is done. The profit to the one engaging in this occupation is gained through the commission which is allowed her by the firm of whom she makes the purchases. This must be made very plain to the customer, who will be suspicious unless she knows how the agent is to be remunerated for her trouble. It is well to make an arrangement with the various stores beforehand, that you may know what to expect and where to fill your orders as they come in. As a rule the shopping agent is allowed ten per cent. on all her purchases.

The advertising to be done in this line should be through the papers which have the largest circulation in the country and in country towns. The agent must be able to give good references; if she can use the names of some persons who are well known, she will, of course, build up a good trade much more rapidly. She will also find it to her advantage to send out circular letters. Usually a good list of country names may be obtained of seedsmen for a small compensation. Dealers in agricultural implements can usually supply good lists.

The shopping agent should not, however, depend entirely on country customers. An advertisement in the city papers, offering to do shopping for invalids or for those otherwise prevented from attending to their own purchases or to accompany those who wish to profit by the experience of the professional shopper will, if accompanied by good references, bring trade after a time. But do not expect to hear from your city advertisement at once. As a rule city people do not read such things as country people do, and it takes much longer to work up a trade among them. Cards should also be left in all the hotels, offering your services free of charge to strangers who have come to the city to make purchases. If you make an agreement with the different firms in the city beforehand, they will credit you with a commission on all the purchases made by the people who accompany you.

To be successful as a shopping agent it is necessary to have the faculty of putting yourself into the place of the one ordering as largely as possible. You must be able to comprehend their tastes and circumstances and thus purchase, not what would please you, but what would please them.

JOB PRINTING.

Is there any good reason why women cannot run job-printing offices successfully? There are three bright girls, all compositors, who are quite determined to decide this question for themselves. They are going to take turns soliciting work, and all who know them believe they can succeed in getting all they can do, and that they will do it satisfactorily. They all know how to set type, read proof and "make up" forms. There are parts of the work that are not easy, but there is nothing harder than is undertaken by most women on wash day, and they know by experience just what to expect. They have not yet been in business for themselves long enough for one to feel justified in calling them successful, but already they are more than making expenses.

SECOND-HAND BOOKSTORES.

A man and his wife rented a little house the front part of which was suitable for a shop, and for many years they earned their living by dealing in secondhand books. The man died a few years ago after a long and tedious illness, during which the wife cared for him and the shop too. Since his death she has still kept the shop open, and none of her customers has been able to see the difference in the manage. Her success points the way to one more avenue by which women may seek independence.

POLISHING FURNITURE.

A girl who needed work and who could not find it was given a fine recipe for a furniture polish that was exceedingly nice for pianos, and was taught how to use it. Now she earns a good living by going from house to house, where she polishes pianos and furniture. She also carries a very nice cleaning oil that she uses when she can get work at cleaning the finishing in fine rooms done in natural wood. It is not hard work, although it is somewhat tiresome, but she makes more than an ordinary clerk or typewriter, and works less hours. Then, when she is sick she can stay in her room without being afraid of losing her place, which is always worth taking into consideration when counting up one's gains.

PICTURE FRAMES.

A girl who clerked in a store where picture frames are made became sick and lost her position. Girls were plentiful, and when she recovered she could neither get her old place back again, nor secure a new one ; yet she must work or starve. Then it occurred to her that she was considered an expert in renovating old frames, more especially those of gilt, and that she might earn a living in that way. Procuring the necessary materials, she started out in search of employment. She could mend broken carving by fastening on a certain composition (of which she had learned in the store), in imitation of the pattern, which, when dry, became very hard, and could be gilded or bronzed or stained to match the frame if it were of wood. She found employment in a majority of the homes which she visited, and her strange trade has already enabled her to travel half across the continent.

LACE MAKING.

Lace making as a business is at present monopolized by foreign women. It does not pay as well as the occupations in which activity or strength or an expenditure of money is required, but there is a large class of American women to whom even the small returns from this employment would seem very welcome. The invalid or the cripple whose hands are not strong enough for sewing or knitting or for the heavier work of the household would find in lace making a pleasant occupation. The torchon lace is quite easily made, and sells at from twenty-five to thirty-five cents a yard directly to the customer. Of course, if one must sell it to a dealer she will get less than that. There are few who can make more than a yard a day of even the simpler patterns. A woman living in the city can usually find customers for all she can make without being obliged to pay a commission to the storekeeper or to the various women's exchanges.

Although one could never hope to earn much in a day at this work, the year's work would represent many dollars' worth of comforts, and would be multiplied indefinitely if one takes into consideration respite from the monotony of the sick room or the pleasure of giving to one's friends from what one has earned herself.

MILLINERY BY THE DAY.

There are many girls who understand millinery and are quite capable of doing it satisfactorily who cannot obtain work in any store. To such, millinery by the day might prove a solution of their difficulties. Where one has many friends and acquaintances considerable work may usually be obtained through them; otherwise one must depend entirely upon advertising in the daily papers. Advertise just as girls do who want sewing by the day, except that you should state that a competent milliner is willing to go into families by the day for a certain remuneration. There are many women who have good material stowed away which they would be glad to use for themselves or for the young girls of the family if they could have the work done at a reasonable rate and in a satisfactory manner. If you understand the trade and have the knack of trimming tastefully, stylishly and with due regard to what is becoming to the face of the wearer, you may undertake to do millinery by the day and be reasonably certain of success.

BIRDS.

In favorable localities a fair living may be made by raising canaries and other song birds. A Western woman obtains all of her Christmas money by the sale of her canaries, of which she has many varieties. The market for canaries alone is limited, however, and if one hopes to earn more than the money needed for Christmas gifts, she should have different birds, and she will find that it will be but little more trouble to place a cage of pet squirrels in her bird store. The ideal bird store has many windows on the sunny side of the house, in which are vines and flowers in bloom, and it is so heated that the temperature may be kept uniform. A bird store will hardly pay in a village or small town, but may be undertaken in a large town or city with fair prospect of success.

PROFESSIONAL NURSES.

Women are the rightful nurses of the sick, and many who wish for employment that will at the same time be something like a "mission" turn to nursing. The field is more crowded now than it was a few years ago, still there is always something for the first-class nurse to do. The wages received vary from six to twenty dollars a week, much depending upon the ability of the nurse and the severity of the case to be cared for. When engaged in a private family the nurse's board is free, and at no time is hers considered the work of a menial. Indeed, it is more apt to be thought that of a ministering angel. As a rule, the nurse wears simple gowns that can be washed frequently, and, when busy a large part of the time her other clothing gets little wear, so that the money she earns need not all go to dress, as it often does when one works in an office.

Sound health and strong nerves are absolutely essential to the good nurse. She must also be possessed of patience, good common sense and self-control. If she have a trim figure, a light step, a low voice and a merry smile, all these will aid her in getting employment. She must know how to read well, and she should have some knowledge of the topics of the day.

After having decided that she possesses the requisites of a good nurse, and that it is a work to which she should give her whole heart, the next step taken by the woman who would be a professional nurse must be to find a place where she may learn. She should visit the different hospitals in the nearest city and apply for a position. She will probably also be required to pass an examination in the common branches of study, but it will not be severe. However, a girl is supposed to have a good common-school education. She may find that there are a number of applicants ahead of her, so she will be wise to make an application in more than one hospital. She will not receive any salary at first, consequently she should have a good supply of necessary clothing when she enters the hospital and enough money to meet her wants until such time as she begins to receive pay for her services. The matron at the hospital can give a very good idea of the amount that will be required for text books, etc. The text books deal with general nursing, physiology and materia medica for nurses, and it is a good plan for the applicant to study up on these subjects while waiting to be received into the hospital.

In most hospitals the nurse must give three years before she can receive a diploma, and very little is paid until the beginning of the second year. As a rule, hospitals do not care to admit girls for training who are younger than twenty-three years or older than thirty-five. Only about three-fourths of the girls admitted are found able to complete the course. Many leave before the term of probation expires because they see for themselves that they are not at all suited for the work. One who has successfully passed through the rigorous course of training demanded, and has secured her

cleaning establishments for the cleaning or laundering of curtains, and a woman at home could do it at a less price and make money at it. If she should advertise to take the curtains down, mend and clean them and drape them again, she would stand a still better chance of working up a good trade. She should have a good set of curtain frames, for the old substitute of pinning them closely to the carpet takes so long a time that it would eat up all the profits. The curtains should be thoroughly examined, when taken down, not only that the worker may see how much time they will take and set her price accordingly, but that the owner of the curtains may be shown how much work will be required, and that places which barely hold together now will be quite apt to show a rent when the curtains are washed. Then these places should be reinforced before the curtains are cleaned.

The making of curtains should become an important part of this establishment, and a woman with ideas of her own will not be long in working up a good business. She should have a set of tiny window frames made in order to show the different styles of curtains and the manner in which they should be draped. She should not be at all afraid to try materials which are not commonly used in curtains, for every woman likes something original along that line, if it is also pretty and artistic. As a rule, furnishing establishments charge more for making curtains than the work is worth, and they would soon find themselves with but little of it to do if shoppers knew of some good reliable woman who would do it well at a reasonable price. Of course the making and hanging of the silk draperies that go over the curtains would naturally become a part of this business, and must be thoroughly studied by the person engaged in it.

HOME DYEING.

The dyeing of partially worn clothing or of new material to be used in rugs, or that which has been set aside for the rag carpet, is a disagreeable job that the housekeeper always dreads, but it is not so unpleasant when one understands the work so well that there is little fear of failure, or when the work is so planned that one is not called away from it to attend to other duties. It is a wonder that there are not more enterprising women who have not thought to take up this branch of employment as a means of making money. There are women who think no more of dyeing a piece of goods than they would of washing it, and they invariably obtain good results. These are the women who should advertise to do "Successful Home Dyeing." There are a great many women who object to the prepared dyes which are now offered for sale, and which may be used so easily that their sale has become enormous. They complain that goods colored with these dyes nearly always fade, and that some of them are apt to rot the material. They like much better to know what is used in the coloring composition, and one really does not lose in the long run by telling them. In fact, if you mean to build up a good business and be considered reliable you must not use anything which you are afraid to have known. One country woman has made a great many dollars by knowing how to color a nice black with logwood chips. Every one knows what she uses, but no one feels sure of doing a piece of work so successfully as she does, and a great many would rather hire the work done than take the chances. Not only does she color goods by dipping them into the dye, but those which cannot be saturated, such as men's overcoats, she colors by brushing them over with a very strong dye made especially for that purpose, doing the work so evenly that a rusty coat, if not badly worn, looks quite fresh and new.

MUSHROOMS.

Mushroom culture is only beginning to receive the amount of attention it really deserves, for there has never been a time when our cities were so overstocked that first-class mushrooms would not bring a fair price. Mushroom raising is not beyond the strength of the average woman.

The common meadow mushroom is the only one of all the edible varieties that is adapted to culture, but from it a number of varieties have been cultivated by enterprising dealers.

By some, the mushroom is grown entirely in cellars, so as to insure as even a temperature as possible, for that is one of the essentials in mushroom cultivation. One enterprising woman had a cellar dug under the barn, which she used for the purpose. It was well ventilated and frost proof. As soon as the mushrooms appear all the ventilators are closed, for the crop is spoiled, even if slightly chilled. The temperature must not exceed eighty-six degrees Fahrenheit or fall below fifty.

Mushrooms may be successfully grown in sheds or stables or on walls that are well shaded. If you decide to use a wall, you will find movable beds the most convenient and economical, or you may simply fasten shelves on the wall, one above another. One lady raised enough mushrooms in half barrels to supply her family and buy a sewing machine. The half barrels were fitted with strong casters, so it was not difficult to move them from place to place as the state of the temperature made necessary.

It is not at all difficult to raise good mushrooms, and directions for their culture are easily obtained. You have only to decide whether or not you have a place to raise them and a market for them after they are raised. If you do not live on a farm you may be obliged to purchase manure, for the ground must be made exceedingly rich, and that may be difficult, for the manure must be used fresh, that its heating properties may not be lost. The spawn with which the beds are planted is not expensive, and may be obtained of almost any seedsman.

A bed comes into bearing in from six to eight weeks after planting, and will produce an almost continuous crop for four months; then fresh beds must be made, for the mushrooms will no longer be fit for use.

Save your peach baskets for packing purposes if you expect to be obliged to send your mushrooms away, and be sure to send them by express.

WASHING FLUIDS.

A woman living in a busy Western town makes quite a nice little sum of money each year by the sale of washing fluids, borax soaps and bluing, all of which she makes. She has some recipes that never fail, and her articles of merchandise have already acquired quite a reputation. Of course she will not tell how she makes them, but any woman can experiment along this line for herself, should she think of trying to earn money in this way.

COOKING FOR GROCERY STORES.

A woman once supported her family through a severe winter by doing baking for two grocery stores. She began by making mince pies, baking for each store every day, alternating one with the other. The proprietors of the stores furnished everything required for the pies, paying her a certain sum per dozen for her work. She made large quantities of the mince meat at a time, taking care not to mix that belonging to the two different grocery stores. Each of the grocers kept a portion of the mince meat to sell to such of their customers as preferred to make their own pies. Gradually other kinds of pies, ginger snaps, cookies and cakes were added, and, although all the family helped about the baking, it became necessary to hire a girl.

There are many grocers who keep cooked food for sale, and a large proportion of them would prefer to have that which is home-made if they could make satisfactory arrangements with a good cook.

During the next summer the woman above mentioned earned her pin money by helping one of the grocers care for his fruit, which would otherwise have spoiled. She could not bake for him any longer, for her house was too small to allow of such work in hot weather. But she made his apples into sweet pickles, and on every Saturday night she canned such of his fruit as had not been sold and which would certainly have spoiled before Monday morning. During the following winter he found a good market for his canned fruit, and was glad he had not sold it at a loss on Saturday evening in order to get rid of it.

CANVASSING.

There is no way in which a woman with the right qualifications can so easily make money as by canvassing. One woman, the wife of a poor man, became so much of an invalid that she could no longer do her own work. It seemed quite an impossibility to bear the expense of hired help, and for a time the outlook was gloomy indeed. One day, while talking over the merits of a favorite journal with some ladies who were calling upon her, she chanced to get them so interested in it that they asked her to send in their names when she renewed her own subscription. That was the beginning. The doctor said she must spend a large part of every pleasant day in driving. Why not endeavor to make her rides profitable? A letter received from her a year later contained the following paragraph:

"I frequently make seven dollars in six hours' work, and it really does not seem like work at all. My health is improving every day, and I am not only bearing the expense of a hired girl, as I set out to do, but I have paid my own doctor's bill, and am now paying for a new kitchen with chamber overhead, which we have just had built."

Very little capital is needed to enable one to start out as a canvasser, and no wonderful amount of knowledge is required. You must thoroughly understand the merits of the article you have for sale, and the remainder of your knowledge will be better gained from experience than from books.

The lady just quoted, when asked to tell the secret of her success from a canvasser's point of view, replied: "Be sure to take what women want and what they can pay for. Consider the tastes, condition and pocketbooks of the people among whom you must canvass. If you always take a needful article, and one worth every cent you ask for it, instead of the doors being closed against you, you will find yourself a welcome visitor. Know all there is to learn about the goods you offer. Dress becomingly, smile your sweetest, and decide to leave a ray of sunshine in every home you visit, whether you leave any goods there or not. If you follow these rules you cannot fail."

The world is full of articles that may be profitably sold by canvassers. There is difficulty in deciding just what a certain person can handle, but as a rule no person can decide this so well as the one concerned. Often she has to decide from the knowledge gained by experience; so, if your first venture proves disappointing, don't jump to the conclusion that you were not cut out for a canvasser, but try something else.

One woman of frail health whose home was in Montana sent to a large grocery house for a sample case of staple groceries — teas, coffees, dried fruits, spices, rice, breakfast foods, etc., obtaining permission to act as agent for that house in her community. Price lists were sent her. Then, with her samples, she drove from house to house taking orders. It was not long before she had built up quite a profitable business, for by fair dealing she was enabled to keep not only all her old customers but to gain many new ones among their friends whose orders she had not even solicited.

Another lady in an adjoining village, hearing of her success, wrote to a dry goods firm for samples, and is now making twelve dollars a week selling their goods on commission, in addition to doing all the work for her family of three. She wisely selected samples of goods not carried in the village stores in the West, yet always in demand where there is even a semblance of social life. Her orders are sent in every day, and are always promptly filled because she demands it. If an article sent is not as good as the sample she sends it back immediately and informs her customer, whose faith in her in thus strengthened, why she must be kept waiting. In both cases these women receive a certain percentage from the establishments they represent, and the goods are as cheap to the customers as they would have been had they gone to the store and bought them for themselves. They are commercial travelers on a small scale, the only difference being that they deal directly with the customer, while the commercial traveler brings the manufacturer's wares only to the merchant.

SERICULTURE.

Sericulture is a subject of vast importance to women, since it opens up for them a comparatively new field of labor. It requires but a short period of time, about eight weeks each year, and during nearly half of that time the work is so light that it could be done by any intelligent child of eight years. The work is fascinating, healthful and instructive, and, what is of greater importance, it is possible for invalids who wish to earn something for themselves. One must not undertake it with the idea that eight weeks' work will make her rich, or allow her to live the remainder of the year in idleness.

Good cocoons sell at from one dollar to one dollar and a half a pound, and an ounce of eggs contains between thirty-five thousand and forty thousand. From these about forty pounds of cocoons should be produced. If sold at one dollar a pound, there would be forty dollars for eight weeks' work. While this is not a large amount, most unemployed people would consider it fairly good pay, and to the mother of a family it would certainly be most acceptable.

If there are no children whose time can be utilized in procuring food and doing other parts of the works, and you are obliged to hire help to go on with it, it will certainly not pay you. If you live where good help may be obtained at very low prices, however, there is, of course, less danger of the cocoons costing you more than they bring. For the first ten days one person can care for the moult; after that it would be impossible. That is why sericulture succeeds best when taken up as a family industry.

Cocoons, to bring a dollar and a half per pound, must produce a quarter of a pound of silk each. In this country there are not many that will do that, consequently more cocoons are sold at a dollar a pound than at a higher price.

It is not wise to purchase more than an ounce of eggs to begin with. Better send to the Agricultural Department at Washington, D. C., for them. You will probably be obliged to pay about a dollar and a half.

Do not go into this work at all unless you are absolutely sure that you have a good supply of suitable food for the worms. Professor C. V. Riley, who is considered an authority on this subject, estimates that the worms from an ounce of eggs will eat between fifteen hundred and sixteen hundred pounds of leaves in their thirty-five days of life. If food must be grown for them, plant the mulberry. The Russian variety is the hardiest. Plant shrubs a year or two old, since food may be obtained from them so much sooner. The Osage orange can be used in States too cold for the mulberry to grow successfully. It will grow in nearly all of the States. Both the mulberry and the Osage orange make good hedges and help to beautify the farm. They may be purchased of nurserymen.

Almost any room in your house may be used for a cocoonery, provided it can be ventilated and kept at an even temperature. The ventilation must be good, as the silk worm is very delicate. Tobacco cannot be tolerated in the cocoonery. It will pay you to vacate the room as soon as the eggs are hatched, and until the cocoons are cared for. Have the room perfectly clean to begin with, and keep it as free from dust as possible. If it is not heated by modern methods, you must use a stove, for the temperature should never be below seventy-five or above eighty. Instructions are usually sent with the eggs, but, like everything else, a larger part of one's knowledge must be gained from experience. A most important item is that very little money is needed with which to make a start. Another of equal importance is that the work may be carried on by the non-producers of the family, and what is earned is clear gain.

The Middle and Southern States are best adapted to silk culture. Any land that is rich enough to produce corn will grow the Osage orange; also the white mulberry, but with the latter the climate must be taken into consideration.

If you are a farmer's wife and are looking for some way in which to earn a little money for yourself, consider the possibilities of silk culture. It seems as if American women ought to succeed in doing what Chinese, Italian and French peasants do so easily.

HULLED CORN.

There is an opportunity in nearly all large towns to earn a little money by the sale of hulled corn, for which there is usually a good demand during all but the hottest months. In nearly all our cities the hulled corn vender is already known and welcomed. In Minneapolis the position is filled by an itinerant preacher, who was no longer able to pursue his calling, and he has been heard to say that his family has not suffered by the change, but really live more comfortably.

This is work which a woman can do quite as well as a man. To succeed in it, she must know how to hull corn nicely without having it taste of the lye used in the operation. It is never as good if the prepared lye, for sale at grocery stores, is used. That made from hardwood ashes is most satisfactory. It should be made so strong that the corn need not be boiled in it long to remove the hull, yet it should not be strong enough to cut the kernel. Most of the corn offered for sale is boiled too long in the lye, which makes it soft and tasteless, and always leaves it smelling of the lye, no matter how much subsequent boiling it may receive. Good hulled corn is tender, yet every kernel is whole and firm inv appearance. It does not taste or smell of lye, and none of the kernels is but half hulled. It is tempting to look at, and it tastes as good as it looks; but it requires a great amount of care and attention, and that is the reason we get so much that is inferior in quality. As soon as the hulls are loosened, the corn should be removed from the lye, and washed in many different waters, until no trace of the lye remains, and every hull has been removed. Then it should be boiled in water that is slightly salted until it is tender enough for the table. If offered for sale in glass quart cans, it will oftener find a purchaser than if carried about in a large receptacle from which it must be dipped. It will pay every time to make it look as tempting as possible, and the person who delivers it should be clean and attractive.

PUMPKINS.

The wife of a farmer living a long way from the city makes quite a sum each year by the sale of dried pumpkins. The pumpkins are pared, sliced and boiled as for pies, being cooked down until quite dry, and great care is taken not to let the contents of the kettle become scorched. The pumpkin is then spread on a white cloth to a depth of nearly half an inch and dried in the sun or made into little cakes and dried on platters in the oven. Of course a fruit dryer would enable one to work to greater advantage. When wanted for pies, the dried pumpkin is stewed slowly for half an hour in a very little boiling water and then used as if fresh, and no one can tell the difference.

The lady uses a small, very sweet pumpkin that she calls the pie pumpkin. Probably seed could be secured of any seedsman. She ships most of her pumpkin directly to friends of hers who keep restaurants and hotels. What they do not take is sold to grocers, but brings a much smaller price. She also sells considerable canned pumpkin, a large part of which is ordered through a woman's exchange, where she usually has samples.

Of late she has done a little advertising with a view to working up a mail trade for her dried pumpkin, and there is every indication that she will have all she can do. She offers, in her advertisement, to send enough dried pumpkin for five large pies for ten cents. When she sends the pumpkin she also sends a pleasant little note to the effect that she hopes it will be liked so well that a large order will be forthcoming. The larger quantities are sent by express.

BATHROOMS FOR WOMEN.

Any city of ten thousand inhabitants ought to support at least one well-equipped bathroom for the exclusive use of ladies. Many women object to going to bathrooms run for men, except on the one day in the week that is set apart for ladies, for even the knowledge that there are only lady attendants on those days does not serve to overcome the feeling that they are going into bathrooms frequented by men.

One who thinks of going into this business must have at least a thousand dollars to start with. She will, doubtless, be obliged to either pay rent for some months in advance or to guarantee payment before she can find a landlord who will fit the rooms up for her. Even then she will be obliged to supply many things for herself. If she could own a suitable building in addition to the thousand dollars she could then open up business quite independently.

To be successful, she must know how to give all sorts of baths in a satisfactory manner; also how to select attendants who know their business and will not shirk, for success depends on steady patronage, and that depends on the service rendered the patrons. It is also important that she be a good judge of character, for unless she is able to detect women of the objectionable class and to turn them away, she will not receive the patronage of respectable women, and without it she cannot succeed.

GLOVE REPAIRING.

There is a man in one of our large Western cities who makes a living by cleaning and mending gloves. He goes from house to house collecting them, then he takes them to his room, where he mends and cleans them. As he does his work neatly, returns it promptly, and as his charges are less than those of the regular cleaning establishments, he has succeeded in building up quite a little business.

This is work peculiarly fitted for women, and if undertaken by a deft-fingered woman, who could add the renovating of soiled ties to her work, it ought, in time, to prove remunerative. Like any other business, it is not built up in a day. One should have certain days on which to gather up their work and return it, and a book account should be kept. This will not only serve to prevent mistakes, but it can be used as a reference when seeking new custom among strangers.

SHEEP RAISING.

The raising of sheep requires very little labor that could not be done by women. Sheep do not need constant attention, and with the help of a few good books a start may be made without the knowledge gained from experience. The wise woman will start with two or three sheep, gradually increasing her flock to one ram and between forty and fifty ewes. It is best to purchase good ones, even though the first cost be a little more, and you should consider whether you wish them to excel in the production of wool or of meat. As a rule, sheep having medium wool neither very fine nor very coarse will be found the best for beginners, as they usually require less knowledge as to treatment.

Do not think of raising sheep unless you have at least ten acres of land and money enough to provide warm quarters for your stock. To make the work pay, lambs should appear as early as February, and this is impossible if the sleeping quarters are cold or overcrowded.

SHOP-WORN GOODS.

A widow whose home is in a busy little village is making a comfortable living for herself and her two children by selling shop-worn goods. She has made arrangements with the proprietors of the largest stores in a neighboring city whereby she receives their shop-worn goods to sell on commission. It is not generally known that most stores have many articles that are rendered unsalable to the average customer by having remained on shelf or counter or in a show window until slightly soiled, yet they are as valuable, except in appearance as anything else in the store. Women who do know this often get what they want at a great bargain. At one time the lady referred to chanced to purchase a four-dollar shawl for less than two dollars, simply because it was a little dingy along the crease where it had been folded. All her neighbors tried to purchase it, and she finally sold it for a dollar more than she had paid. This gave her the idea that led to the opening of her little store. It bears the sign, "Shop-worn

Goods at a Bargain," and in it everything may be found from headwear down to footwear, as well as table linens and other furnishings for the home. Her stock in trade costs her nothing. When a box of goods comes from a merchant she opens it, and labels every article with a card bearing the name of the sender and the price at which it must be sold. Her bookkeeping is done so carefully that she can tell in a moment just what she has received from any firm, whether sold or not, and, if sold, at what price. On the first of every month she sends a statement of account to all merchants whose house she represents, and this is accompanied by a check in case she has made any sales.

Such a store might not pay well in a large city, although they are sometimes to be found there; but in a small town, where many of the women do not feel able to go to the city very frequently, it ought to do well.

BICYCLE MAID.

In a certain portion of New York City it is said that there is a business-like lassie who is known as "the bicycle maid." She earns her pin money by going from house to house among the well-to-do class to clean bicycles belonging to the members who do not enjoy the task, and who dislike to take the necessary time and trouble to get them to the shops where such work is done. She carries everything necessary to her work in a black leather bag, and never leaves a wheel until it is put in the best possible order. She understands the mechanism of a bicycle better than many men who attempt the work, and makes it a part of her business to see that every screw and nut is in its place, and that handle bars, saddles, etc., are in no danger of loosening unexpectedly. She charges just what the owner of the wheel would have to pay at the downtown shops, but her customers say that she does her work more thoroughly and that they prefer having it done at home, and so her orders are increasing steadily.

CLEANING LAMPS, SILVER, ETC.

A number of women are now earning their pin money by going from house to house to clean lamps, silver and bric-a-brac. They carry all necessary materials with them — silver polish, soft cloths, brushes, chamois skin — everything — and go right to work without troubling any one. Usually they are hired by busy women who cannot keep sufficient help, but often they are hired by domestics themselves, who would rather pay for having such work done than to do it. They are also hired by domestics to keep house for them for a day or an evening, when something of importance is going on, and they cannot otherwise get leave of absence. Of course they charge more than the domestic would earn in the same length of time, for they consider the accommodation worth paying for.

BRIDE'S ASSISTANT.

A very capable Eastern woman pieces out her income by acting as assistant in homes from which a bride is soon to go. She does the hundred and one things that usually fall to the overworked mother or sister, and many of which are apt to be forgotten in the press of other duties. She sees to the packing and strapping of the trunks, gives the last touches to the costumes, sees that the bride's bouquet is within reach, and superintends the wedding breakfast or dinner — not as to cooking, but that it may be ready at the appointed moment. In short, she does everything that every one else forgets, and saves the mother so many steps that she is in demand wherever she is known, when there is to be a wedding.

FUNERAL INSPECTOR.

A few years ago the papers were telling of the odd way in which a certain woman was earning her bread and butter. She called herself a "funeral inspector." When her services are required she goes to the house of mourning and assumes the whole charge, saving, the family many annoyances. She gives orders for flowers, arranges them, takes messages to friends or relatives who call, invites people to the services, arranges the rooms for the funeral, talks matters over with the minister and the undertaker, sees that the wishes of the family are carried out, and stands between the afflicted family and the world at large. These tasks may be small, but such assistance is highly appreciated, more especially when the beloved one has been laid away, and some one is needed with whom all cares and worries can be shared for a day or two.

There are not many women with the right qualifications to fill so difficult a position successfully. One must have an abundance of tact and a thorough knowledge of human nature. She must be capable, cheerful and sympathetic and able to conduct everything without haste, noise or confusion.

The woman referred to gets most of her work through physicians who know her worth and are glad to recommend her. Of late years, however, many orders come directly from the afflicted who happen to know what she did for a friend in similar circumstances.

CARING FOR PETS.

A young fellow who is obliged to work his way through college conceived the idea of earning money by caring for dogs and birds and other household pets. He washes dogs, cleans bird cages and attends to any pet that should be cared for regularly and is owned by a mistress who would rather pay to have it done than do it herself. Is there any reason why a woman could not do such work? The young man referred to charges at the rate of twenty-five cents an hour, which is a fair rate of payment for work requiring no greater skill.

CUSHIONS AND PILLOWS.

A Chicago man supports himself by making artistic cushions and pillows, cozy nooks and easy chairs. He does his work artistically, and, being inventive and not afraid to follow his fancies, his handiwork is usually sought for and brings a good price. It does not matter to him whether a certain material is fashionable or not. If it strikes him as being artistic he uses it. He finds his market in the department stores and by exhibiting his cushions at the houses of the well-to-do. When he has nothing that quite suits a prospective customer, he does not urge what he has upon her, but asks if he may not bring something made especially for her. His business has grown so that he has decided to hire a good solicitor to take orders and deliver goods.

There is a Minnesota farmer's wife who also makes a little money for herself by the sale of cushions, but hers are not always covered, although she has enough of them that are to supply any unexpected demand.

Some of her cushions are filled with the best of the feathers saved from dressing poultry for market. Others are filled with cotton from the milk weed, or with pine needles, or with the soft, elastic moss that grows near her home, or with dried rose leaves. Whatever may be utilized for such purposes is carefully saved, and her cushions seem to grow without her missing the time spent in filling them. She takes a few with her every time she goes to town to sell butter or eggs, and they find a ready market among women who have no opportunities to gather cushion-filling for themselves. When she rests, she usually busies herself with a bit of fancy work, and it is always a cushion cover of some sort. Only her odd moments are used in this way; but the result is a nice little sum of money that is all her own.

TABLE SPREADS.

A crippled girl earns her money by making table spreads. She is very artistic, and even the cheapest of her table spreads are attractive. She always has a number on hand to show to strangers, and she makes a great many to order. Whenever she sells a spread, she asks the prevailing color of the room in which it is to be placed, for she prefers not to sell it at all rather than have it go into a room where it will not be harmonious.

EMBROIDERY.

More than one woman earns money by doing embroidery, and some support themselves nicely. Three sisters, daughters of a wealthy man who died leaving them penniless, were forced to earn a living for themselves and an invalid mother, and they could do nothing well except embroidery. This they did exceptionally well. They sent out a bright young girl to show samples of their work and to take orders, and they also left some of it at the Woman's Exchange in their city. Finally, they opened a little shop in their parlor, and advertised that they would teach art embroidery for twenty-five cents a lesson. Each lesson occupied an hour. This advertisement brought them more orders, and so they advertised quite extensively during the holiday season. They sent considerable work to the State and county fairs, and always received enough in premiums to more than repay them for their troubles. One of the sisters usually stayed at the fair, to sell the work and to take orders for more.

They bought materials for their fancy work direct from the manufacturers, taking quite large quantities at a time, which made it much cheaper. This was sold to their pupils, as wanted, at regular retail price, which afforded them another little source of income.

DESIGNING.

Women who are artistically inclined, who possess originality and versatility, and who have had enough training to know a good design when they see it, may make a comfortable living for themselves by designing. There is a call for good work and new ideas among the manufacturers of carpets, draperies, silks, paper boxes, wall papers, oil cloths, and, in fact, among all manufacturers who put out figured goods of any description. How shall the worker find his market? By studying the advertising pages of trade journals, where such manufacturers usually place their advertisements. In many instances they can get addresses from the merchants with whom they deal. They must then send a specimen of their work directly to the manufacturer, with an accompanying note to the effect that, if it is accepted, payment at his regular rates is expected.

There is a woman in England who is known as a designer of artistic furniture, and another who is making a success as a designer of costumes for light opera — a field hitherto entirely held by men.

CANDY-MAKING.

There are few mothers but prefer home-made candies for their children to that which is usually for sale in the stores, and there are few kinds of employment for women more attractive than candy-making. It has a great advantage over many other lines of work in that it may be begun on a very small capital.

Four brothers and sisters once wished to make their father a present of a new overcoat, and they wanted to purchase it with the money they had earned themselves, that it might be an entire surprise. But how earn the money? There was nothing they could do, successfully, "except make molasses candy," as the eldest boy chanced to add, for they were making molasses candy in the kitchen while they discussed ways and means. The chance remark gave them an idea. The mother had just purchased a gallon of molasses, and before the children went to bed that night they converted it all into the nicest golden squares of molasses candy, each large enough for one good mouthful. The next morning each took a share of the candy, wrapped it in squares of white tissue paper, and started out to sell it. They visited offices almost entirely, and sold it all at a good profit. They bought another gallon of molasses for their mother, and some for themselves. They also bought peanuts, for they knew how to make nice peanut candy. Every day they went out to sell the candy they had made, and frequently they took orders for a pound or more to be brought the next day. And so it went on. Every day they practiced on new kinds of candy, and they never offered any for sale until they had learned to make it well. When Christmas came they had more than enough money to buy the overcoat, yet they had not the remotest idea of giving up their business, which had grown so large that they were obliged to hire help in the evening, besides paying mamma for wrapping their candies in tissue paper.

There is a lady in Chicago who prepares candies, salted almonds and various sweets for large grocery houses in that city, where they are placed for sale in glass cases, and look so tempting that they sell readily. During the holiday season she has hard work to fill her orders. She also advertises to supply sweets for special occasions, and during the winter season she has many orders from persons who desire to give pink teas, or arrange socials or other entertainments where it is desirable that the bon bons should be of the prevailing color decided upon.

HOME-MADE REMEDIES.

A middle-aged lady, who had been a trained nurse before marriage, was left a widow dependent on her own resources and with small children that made it impossible for her to take up nursing again. She had always liked to prepare salves, lotions, liniments, and other home remedies, and was in the habit of supplying them free of charge to any one who might be in need of them. Now, she determined to turn her skill to account. Her eldest boy was given a nice little basket filled with neatly prepared boxes of salve and bottles of liniment, all carefully labeled, and told that be might have a commission on all that he sold. She also went out herself, when her youngest children were in school, and soon built up a nice little business, for there were many women who would rather hire such work done than to do it themselves. She gathered boneset and other herbs, and made bitters and extracts that many people preferred to medicines that were prescribed by doctors, believing them less harmful. She always told what she put into any of her concoctions, for she knew it would increase her customer's confidence in her, while few would care to take the trouble to make such things for themselves when they could purchase them at a reasonable price.

She had a tiny garden in which she raised as much as possible of the material used in her medicines, and what she was obliged to buy was always purchased in such quantities that she could get a reduction in price.

HAIR WORK.

There is not so great a demand for hair switches, and for ornamental articles made of hair, as there used to be; still a little money may be made in that line of work, and one who likes it will not be sorry for having learned to do it well. One must understand how to make switches, wigs, waves and frizzes, as well as how to make watch guards, bracelets, flowers, etc. One lady began by going from house to house displaying her goods and soliciting work. Now she hires the work done, and spends all her time soliciting orders. When one is not a good solicitor it would pay to hire some one who is to take orders, especially if you can arrange to pay them a commission on their work instead of a salary.

THE COMMERCIAL TRAVELER.

The commercial traveler, who is engaged in disposing of goods by sample, has hitherto been thought of almost entirely in the masculine gender. There is not the least reason why this should be so. There is nothing about the work that cannot be undertaken by a woman, simply because she is a woman. In these days a traveling salesman is needed for almost every trade and business that can be mentioned — indeed, for almost every branch of it.

To succeed, one must first serve an apprenticeship where she may learn all about the class of goods she hopes to sell. A good beginning may be made by obtaining a position as clerk in some store where these goods are made a feature; but while doing the work and accepting the salary of a clerk, the woman who expects to become a traveling saleswoman must do much more. She will find abundant opportunities of increasing her store of knowledge if she only keeps her eyes open and her wits about her, and she will also learn how to deal with people — a knowledge which will be of inestimable value.

This work should not be undertaken by one who is not a good traveler. A salesman is obliged to travel almost constantly throughout the year, and traveling is usually done at night, that the days may be given to work.

Commercial travelers are sometimes paid salaries, but a certain commission on what he sells is usually found most satisfactory to both parties, for whatever the plan may be he is, in the end, paid for his services according to what he can earn.

If you are a good clerk, not afraid to praise your wares, not afraid of work, if you can read character well enough to know just how to meet your prospective customers, if you are independent, wide-awake, pleasant and quick witted, you need not hesitate to start out as a commercial traveler. And you may be sure that you will have a better living and more independence than any clerk will ever be able to command. A good commercial traveler is never out of work. There are not many women fitted by nature for this position, but it holds a good opportunity for those who can avail themselves of it.

THE DAY NURSERY.

"Leave your babies with us, while you go shopping or calling, and they will receive the best of care. It will cost you five cents an hour for each child."

Notes similar to the above were sent out among the residents of a certain Western city. The residents belonged to the better class of working people, for the most part, and few could afford the services of a nurse girl. The woman and her two daughters who sent out the notes had taken care to secure the endorsement of a doctor and clergyman, both of whom were well known in the neighborhood, for they were sure there were few mothers who would trust their little ones to strangers who had no recommendations. Their home was pleasant, and all three loved children, and knew how to amuse them. The day nursery was not opened with the thought that it would afford a support, but simply that a little money might be earned to help the husband and father, who was trying to pay for his home out of a meagre salary.

Women soon discovered that it was worth more than it cost to have their babies cared for while they did their shopping, instead of dragging the little things through crowded stores. Many young mothers were glad to avail themselves of the opportunity of paying calls or attending an occasional afternoon concert that the day nursery afforded them. It did them good to get out, good to get away from the children for a little while, and the members of their families agreed that it was worth much more than it cost.

Was there an unusually hard day's work, or something to be done that required extra care, or did mamma get up with a nervous headache? For five cents an hour baby could be cared for nicely, and one source of worry was removed.

Mothers told each other of this opportunity to rest from baby tending for an hour or two, and soon extra help had to be hired in the day nursery; for, although the mother and the two daughters knew just how to help the little folks to amuse themselves, they could not well manage more than twenty of them at once.

To succeed in this, one must have a house with plenty of room, warm floors and good ventilation. The furniture must not be too good for everyday use. There need not be many toys, but there should be plenty of things to play with — spoons, cups, bells, strings, etc. One must have a genuine love for children, and a genius for gaining their confidence. If possible, one should own a cow, and she should surely know how to make wholesome bread.

The day nursery is an established institution in many parts of the old countries, where they are made necessary because many mothers go out to work by the day. There is a good field for them in this country, and, without doubt, they will one day be established institutions here also. It will be easier to start them then, but they will not pay as well as they will before competition becomes lively.

LAUNDRIES.

A woman of good business ability may carry on a laundry and obtain a comfortable living thereby.

without doing any of the hard work herself, except that which naturally falls to the overseer of any business of importance. This is a business that may be undertaken with a very small capital.

One woman rented a house in the spring, in what she thought a good locality, and hung out her sign, "Hand Laundry." Then she went to call upon such of her neighbors as she imagined might like to hire their washings done during the hot weather, and secured a few orders. She had some cards printed, which she left at boarding houses and family hotels, and they brought her a few orders. She agreed to do a washing, free of charge, for the landlady, providing she would send her custom amounting to five dollars, and this served to arouse her interest and enlist her co-operation. She hired one good, strong woman, to begin with, and gradually increased her force as work came to her. Everything was done well, nothing was slighted, promises were kept faithfully, clothes were cared for conscientiously, and the business grew steadily, making a living for its enterprising manager from the first. To-day she owns a large plant, fitted up with all the latest improvements. Her children attend college, and she owns a comfortable home free from incumbrance.

CHURCH ENTERTAINMENTS.

The modern church entertainment is not usually considered a means of money-making for the individual, yet there is at least one woman who makes a fair living by planning and superintending such gatherings, when they are to be arranged for the object of making money for charitable purposes. As a rule, there are few ladies in the church with the requisite time or ability to superintend such entertainments, and without a competent leader they can never be very successful. It would pay most church societies to hire some one to get up their entertainments, and, by so doing, much unpleasant feeling would often be avoided.

To succeed in this work, a lady should have a great deal of executive ability, uncommon firmness and tact, and a brilliant inventive genius for anything pertaining to entertainments. Not only must she be able to plan new entertainments, but she must have the courage to carry them out, and the enthusiasm necessary to make them successful. She must know exactly what she means to do before beginning on any part of it, and she must know how to put aside interested women of the church, who are full of unasked advice, without hurting their feelings.

A certain lady who had decided, after careful thought, that this was the only work she was capable of doing set herself to work to make a careful outline of a dozen different entertainments. A blank book was devoted to each. She not only wrote out the entertainment, but carefully indexed it, so that she could quickly refer to any part of it. She made estimates on the cost of getting up the various entertainments, and made notes of the number of persons who would be required to take part and what each would be expected to do. She knew about how much of her time would be needed in getting up the entertainment and how much it would be worth, and she was so well up on her items as to be able to give prospective patrons a vast amount of information in a very little time. Then she sent letters to the various churches in her own and adjoining cities, asking if they expected to raise money for any especial purpose during the winter, and offering her services. It took some time to obtain as much of this work as she could do; but she has given such satisfaction wherever employed that her friends have advertised her freely, and she is now a very busy woman. She has a positive genius for training little children, and as they take part in a number of her entertainments, this ability contributes much to her success.

She now gets up a great many entertainments, and is often asked to bring in outside talent. This has led to the organization of a sort of entertainment bureau, of which she is president. She has enrolled a number of artists along different lines, with the price they charge per evening, and a list of their accomplishments. The artist is paid for his services by the church employing him, but it is understood that he pays the lady president of the bureau a certain fee for every engagement she obtains for him.

CURRENT TOPICS FOR PARLORS.

A lady who was confined to a wheel chair by partial paralysis of the lower limbs hit upon a most agreeable way to earn her pin money. She had always been a great reader, and having a bright, original mind and a retentive memory, was well up on all the important topics of the day.

One day remarks dropped by a caller set her to thinking of the vast number of women who were not well informed but longed to be, yet who did not know how to use their limited time to the best advantage. Then and there she resolved to start a class for such women, and immediately she began to lay plans for conducting it. She sent circular letters to most of the ladies whose names she found in the "blue book" when her plans were completed, and soon she had as large a class as she could accommodate.

Her method was simple yet effective. She took up a topic of general interest, and told the ladies all she had read about it, using the greatest care to present each side impartially. Then her pupils were allowed to ask all the questions on that topic that occurred to them, and a general discussion ensued. At the next meeting a review was given, and anything new on the subject that had come up was carefully gone over. Many of the pupils brought note books and all became greatly interested.

This led to the teacher's help being solicited in the preparation of club papers, and finally she had quite a number of pupils whom she taught by mail — sending them lists of questions on current topics, and revising and criticizing their answers.

It made life bright and busy, and well worth living to a woman who could not take a step, and who might otherwise have been unhappy. She was enabled to pay all her own expenses, and to hire many little things done for her comfort that she would never have mentioned had she been dependent upon another's bounty.

COZY CORNERS.

A woman with artistic tendencies earns her pin money by arranging cozy corners for people who can afford to pay for such assistance. She began by making a number of sketches of ideal cozy corners, some original, others taken from the homes of her friends. These she carried from house to house in an album in which they were placed effectively. Underneath each were estimates of the expense of making a similar corner, and this always included her services. When none of her sketches seemed exactly suited to the room under discussion, she designed something especially for it, and so happy was she in her ideas that she had no difficulty in finding as much work as she was able to do.

She also impressed upon the employer the desirability of sending a small photograph of her cozy corner to friends at a distance, and earned a little money taking the photographs and finishing them.

She made arrangements with a firm dealing in curtains, rugs, cushions and draperies whereby she received a ten per cent. commission on all goods sold through her, and this amounted to considerable in the course of a year.

TOILET PARLORS.

A woman who is clearing over a hundred dollars a month by means of toilet parlors opened less than three years ago says that it will require at least five hundred dollars to fit up the rooms and pay expenses until a business is established. This sum will not furnish rooms very elaborately, but will provide the necessary conveniences and a few pieces of furniture for a waiting room.

To be successful in this line of work one must know how to dress and care for the hair, how to give facial massage treatment, as well as how to treat minor skin blemishes, and how to care for the hands and feet. She should serve an apprenticeship with a specialist in skin diseases, then with a chiropodist, as well as in parlors such as she hopes, finally, to open for herself.

In these parlors she will learn how to wash and dress the hair, how to do manicure work, and how to give facial massage. She will be required to apprentice herself for about four months, after which she should work at least a year, on a salary, in order to gain experience. Many women open parlors with no further knowledge of the work than that obtained in other parlors, but they are handicapped from the start, for women frequently want the scalp and the skin treated, and they will go to one who has knowledge along such lines if they can find her.

Sometimes a chiropodist needs an assistant, and is willing to pay for the services of one by teaching, and there are few who will not give practical instructions for a consideration. This is also true of specialists in skin diseases. In addition the student should have a decided liking for materia medica, and should obtain all the knowledge possible on diseases of the scalp and skin. The more a woman knows when she goes into this business the more money she will make when it is once established. She must, however, be exceedingly careful from the start to keep out all women of questionable character, and she must have it understood that her parlors are open to ladies only. On no account must gentlemen be admitted, for there are few parlors opened for the accommodation of both sexes but soon get a reputation that in a short time drives away all self-respecting women.

There are many women who do not have sufficient capital to open parlors, but who make a living by going to homes to give treatments for skin troubles, to care for the feet and the hands, and to wash and dress the hair. They require as much knowledge in the various branches of their work as the women who open parlors, but ten dollars will purchase as many tools as they will need for a start, and they do not have the regular expenses that the parlors involve. Then, if they are ill, they can rest, and not be worried with the thought that the expense of keeping up the parlors is going on, while the rooms remain closed. On the other hand, they must work up a trade by canvassing, as well as by advertising, and until they get a regular line of custom they can never make any sort of an estimate of the amount of money they will have, which, of course, is not satisfactory. Most of the women now presiding over toilet parlors began business by going to the homes of their customers, and there are women who have abandoned the parlors because they decided that there was less care and anxiety for them in doing their work at the homes of their customers.

SCHOOL FOR DRESS-CUTTING.

There are a number of very good systems of dress cutting on the market, and proprietors of them are glad to find agents who will sell them on commission and teach buyers how to use them. The usual way of doing this in cities and towns is to open a school in some convenient location. The pupils are charged a certain sum for instruction, which usually includes one of the charts, for, of course, they are only taught how to cut and fit by that chart. The first lessons should be given on garments belonging to the pupils, and, by the time the school is well established, others come in with dresses to make that furnish work for the pupils. Dresses are, as a rule, made much more cheaply in these schools than elsewhere, and so they are patronized by many to whom money comes slowly. The proprietor of one of these schools can afford to make dresses at a low price, for she gets pay for teaching the pupils, and also gets pay for doing the work on which the pupils learn. In addition to that she has a commission on every dress chart sold. If she is a good business woman, understands dressmaking, and keeps up with the latest styles, she can build up a flourishing business, and furnish steady employment to the best of the girls she has trained. She will need them to help her with the finest gowns brought into the workroom and to superintend the newcomers.

Some women have done exceedingly well in this line of work; others have not done so well, but, as a rule, the fault lay with themselves. A woman who has no knowledge of dressmaking should not open one of these schools and expect to succeed; yet many attempt it who have only the knowledge and experience acquired while learning to use the chart.

LUNCHES.

Serving lunches to the people who work in offices has become quite a usual way of earning money in our larger cities; still it is, as yet, far from being overdone, and an opportunity is afforded one who is a good cook, as well as a good business woman, to earn a little money in this way.

Sometimes the lunches are put up in bags, sometimes in boxes. Usually a paper napkin is wrapped around them, and always they are made to look as tempting as possible. When ready for distribution they are carried to the offices in a large covered lunch basket. There are usually five-cent, ten-cent and fifteen-cent lunches in each basket. The cheapest ones consist of a sandwich and either a doughnut, an apple or an orange, or a piece of cake. The ten-cent lunches usually contain two sandwiches, a piece of cake or pie, a pickle and some fruit, and the fifteen-cent lunches are quite elaborate. Care is taken to have a variety, so that regular purchasers of any of the lunches may not become tired of them, as they would do if the same thing were always served. There are many different kinds of sandwiches, and many varieties of cake and pie, and the profits are not lessened, in the long run, by serving two or three varieties each day, as well as striving to have something unexpected. One woman, whose coming is looked for in many offices, frequently takes a glass of baked beans, or a cup custard, or a glass of apple tapioca, instead of cake or pie, to old customers whom she fears will tire of her lunches. Such food is not as easily delivered, but she finds it no more expensive in the end. She collects dishes one day that were left the day before. Another woman hires a stout boy to accompany her to some of the buildings where she has a number of good customers. He carries a pail of hot coffee in each hand, for which her customers are only too glad to pay. She serves a variety of sandwiches and cookies, but no cake, pie or pickles.

Some women find it profitable to carry lunches to the cars to sell to the passengers, more especially when the cars stop at their station near meal time. As they meet different people every time, they are not obliged to provide a variety, as when serving regular customers, and they can charge more; but, as a rule, there is apt to be more unsold, and they have not the opportunities of building up a business that would have a marketable value.

One woman, living near a large school building, makes quite a little money selling lunches to school children. She tries to furnish food that is wholesome yet attractive, and so mothers do not find fault with her. She usually has sponge cakes baked in little tins, and her pies are not sold in slices, but in turnovers. She is a very busy woman during the periods of intermission, and often her entire stock will be sold out before the youngsters have all been waited upon. In cold weather she makes a cereal coffee that, with cream and sugar, looks like the real article. It is nourishing and appetizing, and the children who can order a cupful of it with their other food feel very important and grown up.

Several vacant lots were to be filled in near the home of a certain woman, and the work was begun on a very disagreeable day. She made a pailful of good coffee and some nice old-fashioned gingerbread, and sent her little boy out to see if some of the men at work on the lots did not want to purchase her impromptu lunch. It went in a hurry, and in the afternoon she sent the boy with another supply. He went twice a day as long as the men were at work, and always found customers. The same men did not purchase each time, but there were few who did not purchase many times, and, without doubt, drank less beer because of the hot coffee. The woman's happy thought helped the family at a time when her husband was too ill to work, and, indeed, for some time afterward, for new buildings were erected on the lots, and the builders proved as good customers as the laborers had been.

WOMEN'S EXCHANGES.

There are many cities where there is no woman's exchange, and few where one might not be opened to advantage. They are usually started by a number of women, who form a sort of syndicate, elect a board of managers, rent a building suitable for their purpose, and hire the help necessary to carry on their work; but there is no reason why they could not be started by one woman alone and made successful, provided she had the necessary means and the requisite qualifications from a business point of view.

In the regularly organized exchanges the members contribute two dollars annually. There is also a ten per cent. commission on all goods sold, but in the exchange started by the private individual this annual fee cannot be expected.

The woman who starts a woman's exchange ought to have enough capital to enable her to pay rent for a suitable store for at least a year. She will need show cases in which delicate articles left with her for sale may be kept away from dust, and she must make provision for heat and light.

If she must start without capital, or with very little, she might rent a window in some store on a business street, where her goods may be displayed. One woman started her exchange in the parlors of her own home, and gradually worked up until she could afford to rent a suitable building, but it was slow work.

In these exchanges women are not charged for leaving their work for sale, but they are obliged to pay a ten per cent. commission on every sale made. The owner of the work puts her own price on everything left for sale, and is told just what she will have left, if the work is sold, when the commission has been deducted. If she puts too high a price on her work the lady in charge of the exchange may offer her a suggestion to that effect, but she has no right whatever to cut the price. The owner of the work may remove it at any time, or replace it with something fresh. In the case of articles of food, they who supply them are expected to bring fresh goods every morning, and take away that which remains of the amount bought the day before.

As a rule, a lunch room is opened in connection with the woman's exchange, which affords a market for a considerable quantity of the edibles left for sale.

As will be seen, the woman who opens an exchange really opens a store for the sale of home-made goods, but with one difference — she is not obliged to pay a cent for the stock she displays, and she only becomes responsible for it to a limited extent. In case of fire, or theft, she does not replace the goods lost, and she must always make this plain to every one leaving merchandise in her keeping. Of course she is expected to take reasonable care of such goods. It is to her own advantage to do so, just as it is to be agreeable and obliging under all circumstances for, if other women should refuse to leave things with her for sale, she would soon be obliged to shut up shop.

HOUSE-CLEANING.

In some cities regular house-cleaning brigades have been organized, and it is said that, in every instance, they find plenty of work to do during the spring and fall, and at other seasons of the year are kept fairly busy making newly-finished houses ready for habitation.

They provide opportunities for energetic women who wish to go into business for themselves.

One of these brigades was organized by a frail little woman who could not spend half a day in washing windows, no matter how high a price she might be offered for such services, but she knows how such work should be done, and she is so businesslike that she never fails to impress that fact upon others.

She had a little money to start with, and this was spent in sending out circulars and in advertising in the local papers. She found thoroughly competent help who were willing to work for her by the day until such time as she could give them steady employment. She went to two women who were well known and whose recommendations would be of use, and offered to clean their houses free of charge, if they would write letters that she could use in her circulars, and she explained that she would not expect the letters at all if they did not find the work entirely satisfactory. It is needless to add that she got the letters and used them to advantage.

She sent out her circulars, and, while waiting for them to bring returns, she took the letters, put on a pretty business suit, and called upon the mistresses of well-to-do homes, soliciting employment. Her work was not in vain, and now she has all she can do without soliciting.

When given a contract she immediately makes a memoranda of all that is to be done, and decides just how to push the work so that the owners of the house shall suffer as little inconvenience as possible. Her force consists of a paper hanger, a painter, a man who whitewashes or kalsomines, men who beat and clean carpets, men who make a business of repairing furniture, and both men and women who do the general work of cleaning. She will not have a person in her employ who does not take pride in his work or who cannot do it well.

She has several one-horse wagons, and a laundry and cleaning establishment. When she goes to a house that she is to clean she takes all the help that can possibly be set to work there, and she knows how to keep quite an army working to advantage. Carpets are taken up, curtains are taken down, and, with all furniture needing considerable attention, are put into the wagons and carried to her workrooms, where skilled help is immediately set to work upon them.

When the house is cleaned the woman who attends to the bric-a-brac, and the men whose business it is to put down carpets, hang draperies and arrange furniture, are sent in without loss of time, and everything is done so quietly, so thoroughly and so expeditiously that even the most fault-finding woman has nothing but words of praise. If a house cannot be completed in a day, care is taken to leave it as comfortable as possible for those who must spend the evening there.

This woman is considered so reliable that many wealthy families give her the keys to their homes when going away for the summer, and she covers the furniture and puts everything away after they have gone, and gets the house in order for them before they return.

So well does she manage that she can really clean a house more cheaply than it can be done if superintended by its mistress, and so she is bound to have enough to do. She will not be persuaded into taking more than she can do well, nor does she make promises that she cannot keep. No matter how many houses she may have on hand at the same time, she always manages to give each her personal supervision for a long enough period of time to enable her to be absolutely sure that everything is going on all right.

REFRESHMENT STANDS.

The bicycle craze has opened up a line of work that is at present appropriated almost entirely by men, yet it is work particularly fitted for women. It is that of supplying refreshments for weary riders. To be successful one must live on a road much frequented by bicyclists, or must be able to build a stand there. On one of the beautiful roads leading from Minneapolis to Lake Minnetonka there stands a little cottage known to bicyclists as "the half-way house." There is no sign to distinguish it from other houses, but one rider has told another about it until it has an established reputation as being "a fine place to get a glass of milk, or an excellent cup of coffee and a sandwich."

A woman who knows how to make a cup of first-class coffee, who serves it on a tray with real cream, and who can furnish a nice sandwich on demand, need not have any other accomplishments in order to be patronized, if she is within reach of any one who is at all likely to purchase refreshments.

Refreshment stands are always to be found where pleasure seekers are wont to congregate. As a rule, the proprietors make a fair living, although no one patronizes them unless it is quite unavoidable, for the refreshments they serve are usually anything but appetizing and their charges are outrageous. Suppose some woman were to start a rival stand. She might advertise to supply only sandwiches and coffee, but if her prices were reasonable and her food good she would not need to advertise a great while before she would have as many patrons as she could well supply. This is, at least, a method of money making which is worth considering, in case you have tried other methods in vain.

BEE KEEPING.

It is, comparatively speaking, but a short time since bee-keeping has been looked upon as an industry to be studied. In olden times it was believed to be ruled by chance. If one's luck were good, he had honey for his table; if not, his bees died. Now, it is known that money may be made by keeping bees, and that success depends upon knowledge. Literature on the subject is by no means scarce, and good journals devoted to apiculture have an increasing subscription list. Modern methods have increased the supply of honey, and the price is lower in consequence, but the world is by no means overstocked, and good beekeepers will tell you that the profits to be made from bees are just as certain as those from wheat or cows.

It is surprising, when one considers how light the work is, that there are not more women who have turned to apiculture as a means of obtaining pin money. Beekeepers who make money, yet who are considered conservative in their estimates, say that seventy pounds per hive is a fair average. Multiply this by the price per pound, as it is to-day, and you can form something of an idea as to the number of hives you must have in order to make a living.

You will find it wise, however, to begin with one or two hives, and work up as you gain in knowledge and experience. Begin by reading the best books on the subject, and by subscribing for one or two of the best journals. One year's experience should fit a person of ordinary intelligence to go into the business on quite a large scale.

It is wise to purchase good bees at the start; then, if it is not convenient to buy more, when the stock is to be enlarged the beekeeper may easily devote the energies of his hives to an increase of stock instead of to the production of honey. Under favorable conditions bees increase in numbers very rapidly, as many as nine swarms being taken from one hive in a single season. It is safer, however, to reckon on but three, and then you will not be likely to suffer disappointment.

Better begin in the spring, when your only outlay will be for but one or two hives of bees, as you can afford. Do not let any one persuade you into getting more than two hives to start with. You can learn as much as you could from a larger number, and you are not in danger of being obliged to pay so high a price for your experience. Before going into the business you must decide where you will be likely to find a market for your surplus honey, and what it will cost you to market it. You must also know how far your bees will have to go for food, and whether or not they will be able to return the same day. Then you must consider the question of wintering them, and must subtract from your estimated profits the amount necessary to feed your stock during the months when they cannot feed themselves. And you must have a good idea of the amount of money you will need for the purchase of hives, frames, smokers, honey extractors and other necessary paraphernalia. All this may be learned beforehand, and any woman who goes into bee-keeping without a knowledge of such things is very foolish, and will doubtless meet with losses and vexation, as she deserves.

If you live within reach of a library you can get books on the subject without difficulty. If you are miles from a library, and have little with which to buy books, and do not know what to buy even if you have the money, write to your home paper, enclosing a stamped envelope, and ask the editor to tell you of some journal devoted to apiculture; then send for a sample copy. If you like it subscribe for it, if you cannot hear of a better one; subscribe whether you like it or not, and wait until you are better informed on such subjects, when you can easily select one to take its place. Among the advertisements you will find names of parties who deal in supplies for beekeepers, and a letter will bring you any amount of information regarding prices. Do not go into this work, or into any work, for that matter, hoping that something will happen which will enable you to meet expenses as they are forced upon you. It is wiser to know beforehand where the money is coming from, and to have a little sum laid aside to meet expenses upon which you had not counted.

CARPET WEAVING.

The weaving of rag carpets is not the easiest of employments, but many have found it a reliable source of income.

Weaving is easily learned. Good, second-hand looms have been bought for ten dollars, and, without doubt, may be purchased as cheaply as that now if the party who wishes to buy can only find the party who wishes to sell. Insert an advertisement in the dailies of the nearest city for a few times, giving your address, and you will be likely to hear of a loom for sale. If you know enough of the work to be sure of the style of loom you want, it is a good plan to have one made. Before doing so, however, pay some good weaver to teach you all she knows about the work. Have your loom so constructed that you can weave rugs and silk portieres as well as rag carpets, and you will be more sure to have steady employment.

There are few women who ought to attempt this as their only means of livelihood, for it is back-breaking work when continued hour after hour. As a means of earning pin money, it is not to be despised.

A woman undertaking this work should know how to do all sorts of weaving where rags are used for filling. She should always have rags on hand to sell to the women who have underestimated the amount needed, and she should also have a little warp of each color that she can supply, for it will often save time and annoyance on her part, and earn the gratitude of her customer.

A handsome rag carpet seldom lacks purchasers in house-cleaning time, more especially if made with a border.

One woman has taken enough cash premiums at county fairs to pay for her loom twice over, and at every fair she has sold the rugs and carpets that drew the prize at a good price.

Her prize carpets were all made with handsome hit-and-miss centers and striped borders. The center showed but few colors, which, of course, involved considerable dyeing of rags; but the results more than repaid her for her trouble.

Of late years looms with fly shuttles have been invented that are said to enable one to weave much faster; but of course they could not be purchased by the beginner who has but a small capital.

SELLING ON COMMISSION.

There are wholesale firms that make a practice of sending out their goods to be sold on commission, and they are always glad to get names of reliable parties living in communities where they are not represented who will undertake to sell for them. In a book like this it is not advisable to give names of firms doing such work. One who desires to sell goods on commission should purchase a copy or two of some trade journal devoted to the class of goods which they wish to represent. They will find in it any number of advertisements of wholesale firms, and they should then send letters to a dozen or more of these firms, asking if they send out goods to be sold on commission and stating that the writer would like to represent them. A stamped and self-addressed envelope should be enclosed with each letter. Unless a person can give good references as to her reliability and can say so in her letter, she will not be likely to get goods, but with good recommendations she can obtain enough goods to stock a little store.

At the beginning she will find it to her advantage to take samples of her goods from house to house, for in that way she will be enabled to work up a trade much more quickly. Many firms send a handy satchel upon application, in which their goods may be easily carried about. Even when customers begin coming to the store it is well to go out with goods at stated intervals, for there are many women who would buy if they could see them, but who seldom get away from home.

You will soon learn what goods sell best and what firms you can deal with most satisfactorily. This is a means of money making best adapted to villages, where the local stores keep a meagre stock and where there are enough women to give a fair patronage. Women's underwear, dainty neckwear, and, in their season, pretty holiday gifts, usually sell most readily.

Most of the wholesale houses will require you to send in a statement at the beginning of each month, accompanied by the cash, for all sales you have made during the month, minus your commission. If this is attended to in a businesslike manner and you make good sales, you will soon be in a position where you can control several hundred dollars' worth of goods without having a penny invested in your stock.

MASSAGE.

Doctors say that there is bound to be a steadily increasing demand for women who can give good massage treatments, for every day the common people are becoming more alive to its importance as a curative measure. In any sanitarium or hospital of importance it forms a part of the treatment, and very often a physician outside of these institutions sends a patient to them because he does not know where else he can get satisfactory massage treatments.

Massage consists in rubbing, spatting and pinching the body, but it must be done in such a way as to strengthen and nourish the muscles, nerves and fibers and to accelerate circulation. It cannot be done satisfactorily by one who has no knowledge of hygiene and anatomy. It should not be undertaken by any woman who is not strong, healthy and of a cheerful nature. A woman who has a great deal of undefinable force called magnetism will be likely to have most patients, because she will always send them away feeling better than any one else can make them feel.

Some years ago a certain woman was told that she had a great deal of mesmeric power, and would make a fine magnetic healer.

"I'll do it," she replied, promptly and decisively, although the idea had never before occurred to her. "I'll be a magnetic healer, but I'll not be a fraud."

She went to a woman who gave massage treatments and learned what she could there; then she went to a school of osteopathy, where she also took a course. To-day she has handsome private parlors and more patients than she can possibly treat.

Physicians are always glad to hear of a woman who knows how to give good massage treatments, and when you have once learned your trade, you must, as soon as possible, try to see all the physicians in the city where you mean to locate and ask them to send you patients. They will be only too glad to help you if you can satisfy them as to your ability.

Massage is usually taught in hospitals and sanitariums. They who give treatments in their own room sometimes piece out their incomes by taking pupils for private instruction. If you wish to go into this work and do not know where to go for lessons, or whether you would be likely to succeed in it, you would better have a talk with your physician about it. Without doubt he will be able to tell you where to apply.

There are women who seem to be well fitted for such work, yet they do not succeed, even after having acquired all that can be learned without practice. It is difficult to see why they fail. It is simply because sick people do not like them, yet no one can tell the reason of their dislike. If you are one of the people whom sick people enjoy having about them, you need not be afraid to learn to give massage treatments with a view to earning a livelihood thereby; but if sick people do not like you, better try something else, for they will not feel any more comfortable when with you, no matter how much you may have learned. You may as well accept the fact that you have been born without that something which makes them feel better, and, although they may like you ever so much when they are well, they will always prefer that you should cut your calls short when they are ill.

It usually costs nothing but one's time to learn at sanitariums or hospitals how to give massage treatments. Before undertaking it one should have enough means to buy necessary clothing and to pay expenses for the five or six months that usually elapse before work begins to come in.

COLTS AND CALVES.

That a woman may succeed in stock raising has been demonstrated too many times to need further affirmation here. While there are not many who are so situated financially and otherwise as to be able to go into it on a large scale, there are few farmers' wives or daughters who may not earn a little pin money for themselves by raising some of the domestic animals. It may be objected that there is no longer any money in stock raising, yet it is a fact that there are many who are making money in just that way. It is true that the time has passed when one can get a hundred dollars for a very ordinary colt and two hundred dollars for a yoke of oxen, but there is still something to be made if one goes at the work intelligently. With lower prices, greater intelligence is required. A few years ago it paid to raise stock in a haphazard fashion; not so to-day. One must study the work and know what food will make the best stock with the least expenditure of money. A woman undertaking this line of money-making must know what stock will thrive best in her locality, and what will pay best for her purposes. If she wishes to raise cattle for beef, she will not make the same selection that she would if milk or butter were her object. If she decide that she can sell a draught horse more quickly than a driving horse, she will choose her stock accordingly.

A few years ago a woman living on a Western farm wished to visit her old home in the East, but there was no money for the purpose and no prospect of any for some time. About that time a puny little colt came into the world — so puny that her husband decided to kill it.

"Don't do that," pleaded the wife. "Give it to me."

"What can you do with it?" he asked.

"I'll get it to take me for a visit to my old home," was the prompt reply, and the colt's life was spared.

When the mother was in the fields this little colt was fed nice, sweet, warm milk. It took much time and patience to teach him to drink, but the woman persevered, knowing that it was necessary to keep the colt growing as fast as it could during its first years. When the colt was a year old he was sold for a hundred and ten dollars, and the woman went to visit at her old home. While few colts of that age will bring a hundred and ten dollars to-day, yet a good colt will bring something, and that will be found better than nothing to the woman who has no other way of making money for herself.

The woman who has a constitutional fear of horses will do better to depend upon the raising of calves for her pin money. There is no young creature on the farm that is more attractive than a little calf, and they really do not require much of one's time. Like the colt, they should be kept growing nicely, yet they must not be overfed. A calf that becomes stunted from lack of sufficient food or from illness caused from over-feeding, will never quite regain what it has lost. Judgment must be used, and there must be close watching and careful study of each little calf, if each is to be made to do its best. No hard-and-fast rule as to food and general care can be given, for there is nearly as much difference in calves as there is in children.

One enterprising woman, who was a music teacher before marriage, says that she never in her life made money more easily or pleasantly than she has during the past few years since she began raising calves for sale.

Another woman, whose husband is a farmer, had considerable to contend against at first, for her liege lord did not believe there was any money to be made in stock raising, and he said that he had no time to give to it anyhow. The wife finally obtained permission to try it, provided he should in no way be troubled in the matter. With money she had put into the bank before marriage she purchased four cows. She bought the hay and grain they required from her husband, paying what he could get for it elsewhere. She hired a strong girl to help her about the house, and the girl did the milking. Enough butter and home-made cheese were sold to more than pay the girl. At first there was not enough to pay for the food her cows ate, and she was obliged to run in debt, but a careful account was kept, and in the end every cent was paid, with interest. Now her husband is often heard to say that his wife's business is more profitable than his own, yet he has not been deprived of any home comforts because of it.

TYPEWRITING.

Many bright, young girls, who do not enjoy working in an office on a salary, find that they can care for themselves nicely by opening offices of their own, where they do typewriting by the piece. Besides having a good education and a fair amount of business ability, one who expects to earn a living in this way should attend a business college long enough to become expert in stenography and typewriting. A knowledge of bookkeeping will not come amiss, for one should be able to keep her own accounts, and to send out bills in a workmanlike manner. Too many undertake to do typewriting before they learn to spell or punctuate properly, or have a clear idea of the use of capital letters. Without doubt they will fail. One woman, who cleared over a hundred dollars a month, said that, of all the preparatory work she had done, she found a year's experience as a proof-reader the most helpful. She had tried bookkeeping and was liked by her employer, but could not be satisfied in any line of employment until she was working for herself.

When one is properly equipped from an educational point of view there still remains the financial side of the question, which must be considered. First, you must have a first-class typewriter, with desk, a comfortable chair or two and a copy-holder. You can often make a beginning by renting a desk room in the office of some man who is willing to take pay in work, provided you have not money enough to open an office of your own at the start. You should be able to pay your rent for at least three months in advance, and you should have a desk, a table, a dictionary and several chairs, beside the furniture which you would purchase if renting desk room only. As you see, you would need several hundred dollars for a start. You will do best to get into an office building where most of the renters are young business men, for they seldom have sufficient business to warrant them in purchasing a typewriter and employing some one to operate it, yet they have a certain amount which they hire done.

At first you will have to send out cards and circular letters soliciting work, and, perhaps, do a little advertising in order to let it be known where you are and what you are prepared to do.

WEARING APPAREL.

There is an old lady in Minneapolis who makes her pin money selling aprons and oversleeves, .which she makes of black sateen. Her customers are found in the downtown offices, where women work. When the weather is too cold or stormy for her to go out she spends her time in sewing, and then, when a bright day comes, she has a nice stock of goods to peddle. She enjoys getting about, and as she visits the same offices two or three times a year, she receives many friendly greetings from those who remember her pleasant old face and are glad to see it again.

In another city, farther south, two sisters are building up quite an industry along this line. They make black aprons and oversleeves for office girls and clerks, gingham ones for housewives, and those of linen for butchers, bakers and waiters in restaurants. They also make the white caps and jackets worn by these men. They make aprons of bed-ticking for carpenters and men who husk corn, sun bonnets and sun hats for women and children, and mittens of heavy cloth covered with buckskin for farmers. Whatever in the line of wearing apparel one cannot find in an ordinary store may be found in their parlor, which is used for workroom and store combined. Part of their work is put on sale in a country store five miles away, part is sold directly from their own shop, and a great deal is sold by them on pleasant days when it is easier to go from house to house and from office to office than it is to stay at home. All their work is well done. It reminds one of the work done by one's mother. Perhaps that is the reason it sells so well.

SARATOGA CHIPS.

Some one has said that, no matter how crowded a line of work may be, there is always a market for that which is made so well that few can equal it. To make a success of any money-making enterprise one must be careful in the minutia, and this rule holds good in the making of Saratoga chips. They are always in demand, and to one who learns the art of making them well there is a fine opportunity to make a good income. Commence on a small scale, and you may increase your facilities as your business increases.

First, notify your friends and neighbors that you intend making Saratoga chips to sell, and perhaps allow them to sample some of your make, persuade them to give you a small order, and then endeavor to procure other orders from each grocer in your vicinity, and make arrangements to supply the Woman's Exchange.

Having arranged this part of the business satisfactorily, proceed to make the chips to fill your orders.

First, buy your potatoes, a few bushels to begin with, directly from a farmer, if possible. You will find that it is more economical as well as much more satisfactory to purchase the leaf, and try out your own lard. You can get it at any meat market at six cents a pound, whereas you will be obliged to pay eight cents a pound for lard which is not nearly so sweet. If tried out properly, there is very little loss in weight.

Pare and slice your potatoes very thin. You can best do this with the slaw cutter. They must be like shavings. Lay them in strong salt water about ten minutes to harden them, then squeeze all the water from them, and lay them on a cloth to drain. Place a large, shallow kettle on the range (a doughnut kettle is nice), fill it half full of lard, let it boil slowly until it is smoking hot, drop in a quantity of your potato shavings, let them cook until a delicate brown, then remove them with a skimmer, lay them on a cloth until perfectly dry, when they may be placed in boxes, pans, etc.

Care should be taken not to brown them too much, as they will not present so attractive an appearance; yet equal care must be taken that they are sufficiently brown, and for this reason you must be quite sure that your lard is just the right temperature. It is a good plan to drop one slice in to test it.

A lady of Indianapolis, only eighteen years old, commenced making Saratoga chips, which were so good that every one who tried them pronounced them the best of any that they had tasted. For a few months her business was confined to supplying private families and the Woman's Exchange of her city She sent samples of her Saratoga chips to wholesale dealers, many of whom became regular customers. She now furnishes them with six hundred pounds per week, and gives her time to directing her business, for the work is done by hired assistants. She buys potatoes by the hundreds of bushels, and, of course, gets them at wholesale rates.

FROGS.

One of the most unique ways of earning a living was conceived by a New Jersey girl, who, for seven years, has supported herself by raising frogs. She taught school for many years, but tired of that and began to look about her for some occupation which would give her steady employment at a better salary. She now owns a bog and swamp farm, where she raises her frogs. It is reported that her frog returns the first year brought her sixteen hundred dollars, and now she is said to be one of the most financially prosperous citizens of the little town where she lives. While this is not a sort of employment that will be likely to attract the majority of those who read this book, yet there may be one who finds in this item the very suggestion she needs.

OFFICE SUPPLIES.

Women in cities sometimes make a very good living soliciting orders for office supplies, such as stationery, typewriter sundries, letter books, etc. They secure a list of several dealers in these lines, who agree to fill any orders they may take and pay the solicitor a certain commission. The solicitor then makes a systematic canvass of the office buildings once a month or oftener, always endeavoring to call regularly, that she may be expected. Although the owner of the office does not get his supplies any more cheaply than he would by going to the dealer for them, he prefers to order through the solicitor, as it saves him trouble. Besides, she makes it a part of her business to see that he gets exactly what he wants, which saves him much time and annoyance. Most dealers allow these solicitors a ten per cent. commission on their purchases.

As will be seen, they cannot make much until they have worked up a large enough trade to give them orders amounting to at least twenty dollars a day. This is not, therefore, the sort of work to be undertaken except in large cities.

TOLIET COUNSELOR.

A journalist interested in woman's work chanced to hear of a young lady, a minister's daughter, who had adopted a novel method of swelling the family income. She was not allowed to take up any of the work which afforded employment for her girl friends, for, being a minister's daughter, all of her father's parishioners thought they had something to say about it, and every such line of work aroused the opposition of some one. Being possessed of excellent taste, she had, since a child, helped her friends to make the best of themselves, and when she decided to start into business as "toilet counselor" it was not difficult for her to get necessary recommendations. She did not advertise, as she would have liked to do, because her father objected, but every one she helped had some friend whom she told, and so her work grew. She charged one dollar an hour for consultation in her office, and fifty cents an hour when she accompanied any of her customers on a shopping expedition. She told how to dress the hair becomingly, what colors could be worn to the best advantage, what style of gown should be adopted, what neckwear should or should not be worn, and what style of hat or bonnet should be selected. Her taste was faultless. She was an artist by nature, and every customer was studied as if she were a picture. She tried the hair in various ways until it suited the face of her customer, then taught her how to arrange it herself, and she showed, by comparison, just what colors and shades of colors were best suited to her complexion, and how prevailing styles could be modified so as to be becoming yet stylish.

Few persons can tell the effect of colors and styles upon themselves, and she found many who were more than willing to pay for such instruction.

Of course there are few who can do this work successfully. One must possess tact to an unlimited degree, for in telling one what she cannot wear there is always the danger of wounding the sensitive by touching upon imperfections which they would prefer to believe are really not very noticeable. One must know how to seem to ignore the imperfections and teach her lesson by emphasizing the good points, yet she must be firm and stick to what she knows is really the best interests of her customer or she will very soon lose her patronage.

DIRT BY THE BUSHEL.

Although women are supposed to have a natural abhorrence for dirt, there is at least one woman who has discovered that she can sell it for fifty cents a bushel and thereby obtain her pin money.

It is often difficult for the city housewife to get good soil for potting plants, and when it is brought right to her door she considers herself fortunate, even though she is obliged to pay for it.

The woman who sells dirt has a light market wagon, and carries her supplies in neat wooden boxes with covers. These boxes are carefully labeled, for there are different mixtures, suited to the needs of different plants. When requested to, she will fill the pots and transplant the flowers, for which work she charges at the rate of thirty cents an hour. This is, of course, in addition to the price of the dirt used. The price may seem high to some, but when one realizes how many plants can be repotted in an hour by a deft-fingered woman, one never feels that she has reason for complaint.

All the plant soil sold by this woman is subjected to a baking process that rids it of insects injurious to plant life. The woman who loves flowers in her home will find it difficult to say no to the woman who comes to her door with just the food her plants require, more especially when it may be purchased so reasonably, and she will be likely to give an order for dirt to be delivered at least once a year — twice a year if she raises many plants.

RUGS.

A certain woman is known for many miles around the locality in which she lives as "the rug woman." She has always had a mania for rug-making, and eagerly seeks information regarding new styles in home-made rugs. It would really hurt her to know that any woman could make a rug that was in any way superior to hers, or that was in a style which she could not copy.

She has a loom on which she weaves very handsome rugs, but her sheepskin rugs sell most readily. Her husband owns a sheep ranch not many miles from the town in which she lives, and all of the pelts of the sheep that die during the winter are given to her. It is hard work to prepare them for rugs, but she does it with the assistance of one strong woman and a boy. She finds the work far more satisfactory if she superintends it herself. When the skin is well tanned, soft and sweet, and the wool clean and white, a part of it is dyed in pretty and substantial shades. Some of her sheepskin rugs are all in one shade; others are composed of strips of different colors sewed together, either for an entire rug or for a border on a rug, the center of which is one color. Many of the rugs are made entirely of small pieces of sheepskin, colored and sewed in blocks like old-fashioned quilts. These have two advantages — one is their novelty, the other is that the small bits left from other rugs may be utilized.

These sheepskin rugs wear almost indefinitely, and are pretty for couches or for the invalid's chair. They clean easily and sell well.

This lady also weaves rugs of old carpeting that are warm, durable, and much sought after by the artistic. When soiled they have only to be hung on a clothesline, where they may be played upon by a garden hose until perfectly clean. Either ingrain or Brussels carpeting are used in the manufacture of these rugs. They can be made to order by her from one's old carpeting for a certain price per yard. She also purchases second-hand carpeting, when she can get it for a song, and makes handsome rugs, which are for sale at her home or in the stores where she has made arrangements to place them, or through the agent who now travels for her constantly.

She has old-fashioned braided rugs which sell well, drawn rugs for which there is a fair market, and other varieties which do not sell at all, because they require more work than they are worth. But they serve to furnish her salesroom and attract the curious, and so she considers them of value from a business point of view, since they help to advertise her as "the rug woman," and, in this day of specialties, that is no small matter.

TAXIDERMY.

It is said that of the many avenues now open to women, taxidermy has been entered by the fewest; yet, to a certain extent, it is found profitable as well as pleasant. To make it successful from a financial point of view, one must understand how to dress skins as well as how to stuff and mount specimens, and, of course, one who is located where hunting is good will do better than one who lives in a place where game is brought from a distance.

There are several very good books from which one may learn taxidermy; but, if possible, there should be many weeks' practice under the instruction of a practical taxidermist. Any one having patience, deft fingers, precision and a love for the work may learn to do it acceptably. To do it exceedingly well, one should have a good knowledge of natural history, and should be a close student of animal life. In no other way can lifelike effects be obtained.

It is believed that the work of the taxidermists should be seen more frequently than it is in all buildings devoted to educational purposes, and that it would be if there were more good taxidermists who would dispose of their work at reasonable rates and interest themselves in trying to dispose of it. At present the taxidermist expects his customers to come to him. This is an age when the producer seeks the purchaser, and the enterprising taxidermist, who can convince the school board of the advantages of having practical illustrations to the lessons in natural history is the one who is going to make her business pay.

MENDING BUREAU.

Four girls, all of whom understand how to do fine needlework, as well as that which is more practical, opened a mending bureau. One made a specialty of putting new facings and bindings on dress skirts; another mended underwear; a third devoted herself to repairing coats, cloaks, basques and men's wear, and the fourth mended laces, gloves, fine table linen and dainty trifles that are usually thrown away when torn, because there are few who know how to repair them nicely.

The girls had cards printed which they took turns in distributing. At first all but one would go on what they called "a distributing tour," but as work began to come in they had less and less time for this part of the business.

They were pleasant, obliging and ladylike, and they often brought work back with them from their "distributing tours." They never failed to make friends who, if they could not give them work, were very glad to recommend them to others, and the girls soon saw that they were right in the belief that there were as many who were glad to pay for having their mending done as they were glad to do it.

There are mending bureaus in a number of our large cities, but it is safe to say that there are many such fields still unoccupied, and in some of the very cities where there are capable seamstresses suffering for work.

FOOD SPECIALTIES.

Not long ago the papers were telling of a businesslike woman, living near a thriving Western town, who makes a good living selling mincemeat, fruit cake, head cheese, sausage and Hamburger steak. She began by making tiny mince pies, which she left at the houses where she hoped to find customers, stating that she would like to have orders, and at what prices she could fill them. At least two-thirds of those who had received samples ordered some of her mince pies or her mincemeat. When she delivered it she sent with it samples of her fruit cake, with a note saying for how much per pound she could make it. And so she worked with each article of food that she proposed making. If a housekeeper failed to order either mincemeat or fruit cake she left a sample of something else next time, and there were few of those upon whom she called from whom she did not get an order for some of her specialties. Whatever she undertook she did exceedingly well. None but the best materials were ever used. She was an excellent judge of groceries and meats, and seldom had anything inferior offered her. Then she always bought by the quantity, and so paid less than housekeepers usually pay for poorer articles.

To succeed in this work one must be a fine cook, a good judge of foods and a fine business woman. One who is easily discouraged will not be likely to work up a very large trade. A strict book account of all transactions should be kept and a scale of prices prepared from which there must be no deviation.

Except in special cases it will be found that, if cash payments are insisted upon, they can be met by the customer, and there will be less danger of difficulties than where the credit system is followed.

To begin as the lady above mentioned started necessitates the giving away of considerable food until a trade is established, but it is really a cheap way of advertising, and pays in the long run.

TOWEL EXCHANGES.

In any enterprising town of eight or ten thousand inhabitants a towel exchange may be run with profit. A woman who has tried it gives her experience as follows to the editor of a progressive periodical devoted to women:

"We bought a towel rack and two and one-half yards of toweling, made a roller, put it on the rack and started. Many of the proprietors of stores and offices had never heard of such a thing as we proposed. I would unroll a towel, telling them at the same time that I intended starting a towel exchange and would be pleased to furnish them with clean towels at a reasonable rate.

" 'Oh, do you want to sell that? How much do you want for it?'

" 'No,' I would reply, 'this is not for sale. Here is the idea. I will put up one of these racks in your store and put a towel like this on it once a day, or every other day, as you prefer. I will send a boy who will remove the soiled towel and put a clean one in its place. Thus you will always have a clean towel, which is something every store should have.'

" 'How much do you charge?'

" 'Well, for a clean towel every day I shall charge twenty cents a week. For one every other day, fifteen cents a week.'

"The reply almost invariably was: 'You can put my name down and I will try it.'

"We made a success of it, too. I started in with cotton toweling at five cents per yard, and gradually changed to linen. My husband and I washed every morning, and as soon as the towels were almost dry we would fold them up nicely and run them through the wringer, which made them almost as smooth as a hot iron could have done. We got a child's express wagon, large size, put a box in it with hinges on the lid, and divided it into two parts — one for clean, the other for dirty towels. My thirteen-year-old brother made the rounds with it every morning before school.

"Of course the newspapers wanted their pay taken out in advertising, so we had an item in the local columns of two papers. That helped to make our work known. The butchers wanted theirs taken out in meat. That suited us, too. Everything was done on business principles. I had printed statements and would make out the bills and present them every week, marking them paid as I received the money. I carried on the business for three months, and then sold it to a woman with a large family for just what the towels and racks cost me. In that time I had cleared over sixty-five dollars. This amount, understand, was what I cleared, for I had, besides, made the cost of the toweling, racks, soap, etc. I should not have sold out had we not been leaving the town.

"The towel exchange in cities grows to be a big business, demanding considerable help and numerous teams and wagons to do the delivery and picking up but it can be worked in smaller towns quite as well. On my list I had printers, butchers, blacksmiths, wagon-makers, grocers, dry goods merchants, plumbers, photographers, lawyers, doctors, bakers, confectioners, moulders and barbers, besides several public school buildings. I had plenty of spare time for my other work, and the comfort of knowing that, although we were obliged to work hard for our living, we were succeeding in making our expenses."

What has been done can be done again, and the above experience ought to encourage a great many with whom the financial outlook now seems hopeless. A start may be made with a comparatively small amount of money, and the work is really not very disagreeable, for, in these days of excellent washing fluids, soiled towels may be laundered with comparatively little labor. If it is possible to begin with the linen toweling, it is wise to do so, because it is much more easily laundered and wears longer, which, of course, is a saving in time and money. There are many places where racks need not be procured, for towels a yard in length are preferred to the roller towels. One would, of course, be obliged to furnish more of them at the same price than of the roller towels.

PHOTOGRAPHER'S SUPPLIES.

A businesslike girl in a Western village fitted up an unused shed belonging to her father and put in a stock of photographer's supplies. She obtained these supplies from a friend in the city, who was willing to let her have them on commission, and so she was enabled to open her store with quite a nice stock of goods which had not cost her a cent. As her rent cost her nothing, her parents could not oppose the venture, although they did not believe she would make enough to pay for her time. Her home was situated on a corner lot, in a well-traveled portion of the village, and her sign was plainly visible from one of the streets along which was a fine cycle path. She was an enthusiast on photography, and knew the value of a "dark room" to cyclists some distance from home. Before opening her shop she had learned how to develop and mount photographs acceptably. It chanced that she opened her shop at the beginning of the kodak fever, and, as there was no similar establishment within many miles, she soon built up a paying business, much to the astonishment of her parents.

BAKED BEANS AND BROWN BREAD.

A Boston woman who contemplated going to Montana first sought and obtained employment in a Boston bakery. She worked there for six months, then started out to seek her fortune. It was in the days when female help was scarce in the West and everything advertised as "home cooking" sold for good prices.

She put advertisements in the local papers to the effect that she was prepared to furnish Boston baked beans and brown bread to private families at usual rates, and soon she had all she could do. While a majority of the families preferred to have theirs on Sunday morning, they invariably chose some other day when told that her Sunday list of customers was full, rather than be deprived of her beans and brown bread. She soon had so many of the regular customers who took her merchandise on certain days each week that she could not sell at all to the chance buyers. She did not try to secure more customers than she was able to supply herself without help, for rent was high and servants' wages higher, and she knew that she could not make as much, proportionately, and would have more care and worry by trying to enlarge her business. Her customers always sent for their beans and brown bread on the appointed day, and so she was not obliged to pay delivery expenses. She now owns one of the finest homes in Montana. She was fortunate, of course, in going to Montana just when she did, but the successful woman always owes a large part of her success to the intuition which tells her just when to undertake a new enterprise.

HERB GARDENS.

It is surprising that more women have not thought of herb gardens, when considering how they may earn money that will be all their own. This source of income is open to women who live even in villages, for a corner of the back yard may be made to yield an income that is not to be despised. It is not difficult to raise herbs, and it is really a pleasant sort of occupation.

If you have only the back part of your lot to use for the herb garden you must, of course, make the best of it, whatever the soil may be. If you live on a farm, or where there can be a choice, select good, light soil and have it made very rich with well-rotted manure. If you have but little space you will find it most convenient to plant your herbs rather closely together in beds small enough to allow of your reaching half across them from any side. Have the paths between the beds wide enough to allow of your weeding your plants comfortably. If you are where you can have as much space as you want it is best to plant the herbs in long rows far enough apart to allow of your walking between them on a dewy morning without getting your skirts soiled.

Sage, caraway, coriander, catnip, thyme, lavender, are all perennials, and when once started will not need a great deal of care to keep them growing year after year. A writer of experience on this subject says:

"These herbs should have a good mulching of old manure or compost every fall, which should be turned under in the spring at the same time that the earth is loosened and made mellow around the plants; after this an occasional hoeing or forking over of the soil while the plants are making growth is all the care necessary to keep them in a healthy, growing and profitable condition for several years at least. But as soil often grows tired of one kind of crop, and as the plants may get rootbound and not do very well, it is wise to make new beds and either separate the old roots or raise new plants and pull up the old ones once in a while. However, the conditions of soil and growth are so unlike in different places that each grower must use her own judgment as to when new plants would be preferable to the old ones.

In a small garden it would not be wise to try to raise more than three or four varieties of herbs, but one's choice should depend upon the probable market. One might ascertain at her grocer's or the nearest drugstore for what she would be most likely to find a market.

Upon her list of marketable herbs our gardener must not neglect to put sweet basil, summer savory and sweet marjoram, all of which are annuals. She must also raise parsley, a plant whose leaves are used in cookery and its root as an aperient medicine. There is nearly always a demand for parsley, more especially if it is attractive in appearance.

If one would have a steadily increasing market for her herbs she must use the greatest care in curing them. They should never be cut except in the middle of the day, when the sun has dried them thoroughly. They are best when dried in a cool, airy room, as the sun and wind impair their flavor. It is better if they can be dried without being washed, but this is not always possible.

One woman makes a practice of spreading clean straw around the roots of her plants two or three weeks before she expects to begin cutting, then, when it rains, the sand and dirt are not beaten into the leaves. She packs her herbs in paper boxes when they are perfectly dry, and they look so neat and tempting that they always sell well. A person who purchases of her once is sure to do so again. Each year she fills many small paper bags with herbs and sells them to new customers for five cents each. This is for the purpose of drumming up trade. It does not require much persuasion to get any one to buy herbs when but five cents need be expended, and she knows that the chances are the purchasers will soon be sending to her house for a larger quantity. She has her name and address stamped on every bag.

In addition to her herbs she raises red peppers and the large green varieties of peppers used for mangoes. Of late years she has been experimenting along a line that bids fair to be remunerative. It is in raising boneset, sarsaparilla, spikenard, ginseng and various mints, and the cultivated plant is, in her estimation, far superior to its wild brother. She finds it more difficult to raise these plants than those which have become used to cultivation, but she says it is also more interesting. Her idea is to make liniments, spring bitters, salves, cough syrups and various home remedies whose ingredients are principally roots and herbs.

Her lavender always sells readily. There are still many housekeepers who cling to the sweet, old-fashioned habit of placing lavender blossoms among their linens and in their bureau drawers. Besides, she makes a nice perfume of it, for which she is finding a fairly good market, although she has been at it but short time.

BUTTER-MAKING.

When one has an opportunity to visit at farm houses and see how the butter is usually made, one no longer wonders that there are so few who find butter making profitable. A thorough knowledge of scientific butter-making, applied to the conditions existing in the average farm house, would result in a vast improvement, and there would be less call for creamery products. Many women say they would prefer to buy butter sent directly from the farm, if they could only be sure that it would be good, but, as a rule, buttermaking is carried on in so haphazard a way that, while we find it nearly perfect one week, we know that it is liable to be hardly fit to eat the next.

In successful butter-making there must be careful attention to details, scrupulous cleanliness, and as even a temperature as it is possible to attain. One must have a keen sense of smell, keen sight and deftness of touch. It should be constantly kept in mind that milk is easily affected by a tainted atmosphere, and that good butter cannot be made from tainted milk. One really ought to have a room devoted exclusively to milk if she thinks of making butter for a profit, and nothing else should be allowed in it. It should not be entered directly from the kitchen, for the kitchen odors must not be allowed to reach it, as they would were there direct communication. The ideal arrangement is to have a detached milk house, kept at the proper temperature in cold weather by steam pipes running from the plant used to keep the house comfortable. Of course there are few who can &ave the ideal house. Since butter always brings the best price in winter, arrangements should be made to keep milk and cream from freezing. Some put it into the cellar, but no matter how well built a cellar may be, it never has sufficient ventilation, and the butter acquires an unpleasant flavor in consequence. A milk room can be heated very well by means of a large stove, where the fire is never allowed to burn briskly enough to raise the temperature suddenly or to a too high degree. If a room in the house is to be utilized for the purpose, there should be a little hall between it and the kitchen which will tend to prevent the kitchen odors from penetrating.

One may learn a great deal of the theory of buttermaking by attending the summer schools of agriculture which are held in so many States. In one such school, lately held, a lady who attended all the lectures summed up the essentials to success as taught here as follows:

"Cleanliness and attention to details, the deep setting of milk at a low temperature in a clean atmosphere, ripening the cream at a uniform temperature of sixty-two degrees, stopping the churn at the right moment and washing, salting and working the butter in the granular state."

There is certainly nothing very formidable about them, and it would seem that a woman of average ability, who is gifted with a talent for painstaking thoroughness, might make butter so superior to the creamery products that she would find it hard to supply the demand. Home dairying is certainly found remunerative by a great many women, but they send out a gilt-edged product that does not vary in quality from one year to another.

VINEGAR.

There is nearly always a market for good homemade vinegar, and more than one enterprising woman is earning her pin money by making and selling it. There are many housekeepers who object to the article for sale in the stores, believing that a large part of it is made up of chemicals that are injurious to the health. With this, as with the majority of home-made products, it is better from a financial point of view to seek a market by going from house to house and thus avoid paying a commission. Such a course is more important when finding a market for vinegar than for almost anything else, because housekeepers are slow to believe their grocers when told that vinegar is home-made and strictly pure. If one expects to make a reputation that will sell her vinegar without advertising she must never use chemicals of any sort. She should have different kinds of vinegar for sale, for what suits one is not always liked by another, and there are women who, if offered cider vinegar will be very sure to ask for maple vinegar, or that which has been made of corn or pieplant. When one can surprise them by giving them exactly what they ask for, one is almost sure to make a sale. One woman whose vinegar always finds a good market brings it to town in two-quart glass jars neatly labeled. Each brand is as good as it can possibly be made, and is always what it purports to be. She also makes fine spiced vinegars, which are brought in pint jars. These cannot always be obtained at stores, and she finds many purchasers who are more than glad to buy of her.

CHEESE-MAKING.

As this book is not intended for the woman with money enough to undertake ventures of magnitude so much as for those seeking to make pin money, this article will only offer suggestions to those who have cows and wish to earn money at home by making cheese.

One does not need elaborate paraphernalia in order to make good cheese at home. Buy a good cheese hoop, a clean tub, a good dipper and a boiler. You will, besides, need a pair of scales and an accurate thermometer. In cheese-making you will find that it does not pay to do anything by guess. If you use rennet tablets buy them by the package, and you will then get directions for using them. Do not make the mistake of using more than is called for, or you will have tough cheese. If you prefer, and have calves to butcher, you can save your own rennet. Do not begin until you have read enough about cheese-making to at least know how curds and whey should look. Any good farm journal or domestic periodical can supply you with a back number containing directions for making cheese. Do not imagine that there is no work connected with cheese-making, for it requires a great deal of labor and almost constant supervision, but it. is one of the most interesting of employments.

One woman, whose cheese is always in demand, has only three cows, but before making a cheese she arranges with her neighbors for the purchase of what milk they have to spare on the morning of the day on which the cheese is to be started. She has regular customers in the city whom she supplies with butter and eggs, and many of them take a whole cheese at a time. They like it when it is new, even though it is eaten too quickly to be profitable. She also sells many bowlfuls of the salted curd — an article of food that many people like, but few can purchase, because it does not keep long enough to be on sale at the Stores. She frequently sells the entire hoopful of curd before putting it into the press at all, and she often starts cheese before driving to town with her butter, that she may have fresh curd to take along, for she knows there will be a call for it among her customers.

HOTBEDS.

One energetic woman earns her summer vacation every year from her hotbeds. She says that the beauty at her employment lies in the fact that it lasts but a small part of the year, and she can have the remainder of the time to herself. She has five hotbeds six feet wide by fifteen feet in length. They are very simply constructed. Shallow trenches were dug, and a box frame of heavy planks, about twenty-six inches high at the back and ten in front, was firmly placed in each trench and well banked with manure. Cleats were fastened inside these frames for the support of the glass covers, three of which were fastened on each bed with strong hinges. Having the cover of the hotbed thus divided into three portions, each five by six feet in size, the work of tending the beds was much lighter than it would otherwise have been.

People living in the suburbs of a city nearly always try to have a small garden, and they usually prefer to buy plants to depending entirely upon seed. This is also true of a majority of farmers, who are too busy early in the season to attend their hotbeds. It was among such people that this woman found her market. She soon gained a reputation for selling strong, thrifty plants, and after the fourth year she was no longer obliged to seek a market, for it sought her. She told a reporter that her hotbeds brought her a clear profit of one hundred and eighty dollars during the spring of 1897, and that she might have made still more had she not run short of some plants.

PIGEONS

A nice little sum may be made each year by raising pigeons for market. They sell, in many markets, for from thirty-five to sixty cents a pair, the price varying with the season and the perfection of the birds. They multiply rapidly, and are so easily raised that it is surprising that more women living on farms and in villages have not taken up this method of earning money. You must have an equal number of males and females when starting into this business, for they mate, like all birds. Each pair will raise several families during the year. They usually lay two eggs, then begin setting. The eggs hatch in eighteen days, but they frequently lay eggs for the next family when their first one is less than a week old. They are not at all particular as to nests, but insist on having some place to call their own. Shallow boxes a foot square, with a small opening left for a doorway, answer the purpose nicely. If you live on a farm they will get their own living for the most part, but in villages they must be fed grain. Wherever you live there must be sand, eggshells and broken plaster for them to go to as they like. They also require clay, and rock salt should always be where they can find it.

One woman, who lives in a village, makes quite a nice sum out of her pigeons, although she is obliged to keep them confined, because her neighbors do not like them. She has a large yard, covered and surrounded with wire netting. She is, of course, obliged to be careful as to the cleanliness of the surroundings, for otherwise her birds would die. It is much more work to care for pigeons under such conditions, but she thinks it pays better than it would to attempt to raise poultry in the same amount of space, because they bring more per pair. She has a second yard, also screened in, where the young birds are placed as soon as they leave the parents.

CORSETS, BANDS AND DRESS FORMS.

The success of Annie Jenness Miller proves what can be done by women who have original ideas regarding woman's dress, more especially if they run on lines combining beauty and comfort.

There is a woman in Minnesota who, being uncomfortably stout, set herself the task of inventing a corset waist that would be comfortable, yet shapely. She succeeded in designing something that other women wanted, and, before she realized it, she had enough orders to warrant her in renting an office and hiring help. She next invented an obesity band for women that was considered so good and comfortable that doctors recommended its use for those who were pregnant and who were thereby enabled to get about with greater ease. She next turned her attention to breakfast waists and dress forms, and all of her garments seem to be so well liked that she has as much work as she can attend to.

Another woman designed a corset waist coming below the hips and having buttons on its lower edge to which fasten petticoats. This she carries from house to house, soliciting orders, and, as the garment is especially nice for women with large hips, and is also liked by women looking for hygienic garments, she takes enough orders every day to keep two sewing women busy at her home.

With all that has been done in this line of dress reform, women's dress is yet far from being satisfactory, and there are plenty of opportunities for bright, inventive women to make money designing garments that are both comfortable and artistic. In this day they must be artistic or they will not meet with success. They must be built on hygienic principles, and they must be well made. A person should know how to cut and fit by measurement instead of patterns before attempting to earn money in this way. One who has served an apprenticeship to a tailor will be more sure to satisfy her customers, because she will have had opportunities to learn the necessity of exactness.

GREENS.

There is a woman who has several hotbeds devoted to the raising of greens, besides quite a large garden devoted to the same purpose. She has fine greens for sale before they are generally found in stores, and they always look so fresh and tempting that they sell readily at a good price. Most of them are peddled from door to door by her two boys, who receive a commission on what they sell. Many housewives drive directly to her home, where they make their own selections. Restaurant keepers are glad to buy of her, but she seldom goes to them except as a last resort, for they are not willing, as a rule, to pay what she can get elsewhere.

By applying to her, one may have a choice of spinach, young beets, young turnips, Swiss chard, lamb's quarter, plantain, mustard, kale, nasturtiums, Brussels sprouts, and, in fact, almost everything, wild or cultivated, that any one ever cares to use for greens.

MOTHER'S ASSISTANT.

There are a number of nice old ladies who are earning a living for themselves by going out by the day to take care of babies. They charge fifty cents for a day and twenty-five cents for an evening if relieved by half-past ten o'clock. If obliged to remain until midnight they charge fifty cents. They thoroughly understand the care of young children, and are a boon to mothers who have insufficient help, more especially when there is sickness in the family.

This is a nice field of labor for elderly women who no longer keep house for themselves, but live with their children.

They can make known their willingness to work by leaving their names at the various intelligence offices and by advertising. They must be sure to add that they can give good references. They often find work by telling physicians of their wish to get it, their qualifications and their charges per day. Friends of the family sometimes are enabled to find employment for them, when once they know what sort of work is desired.

CONFECTIONS AND FRUIT JUICES.

One can think of few ways by which a woman, whose home is in a flat, can earn money without being considered a nuisance, yet there is one such woman who has solved this question to her satisfaction, and her neighbors make no complaint. She has built up quite a little business in the making and selling of confections, and this has led, naturally, to the preparation of fruit juices. She has a fine storeroom in the building where she rents, else she could not carry on her work there.

During the season when oranges and lemons are plentiful she candies sufficient peel to fill her orders for a year, and the juice from the fruit is carefully bottled. She makes less on that than she does on the candied peel, so no fruit is purchased simply for the juice, excepting grapes.

She sells a great deal of the grape juice to hospitals, although private parties send in orders, and the grocery stores are glad to handle it for her. Her other fruit juices find a ready market among private families, who purchase them for their medicinal virtues, and at drug stores and other places where there are soda fountains.

Her candied peel and citron are now called for at a number of grocery stores, where it has been kept for several seasons in preference to that put up by any one else, for hers is always good.

She also prepares candied fruits for the holiday trade and for fine parties.

She has nicely printed circular letters, which she sends out to solicit orders, and she is gradually building up a good business. Although she began with confections, there is every indication that she will make more selling grape juice than in any other branch of her work, because its efficacy in illness is becoming more generally recognized every year, and doctors are glad to recommend the purchase of that which they know to be pure and carefully put up.

FARMING.

It has not been many years since women began to realize that there was no real reason why they should not go into farming as well as the male members of the family. Now, farming is one of the first thoughts of the broken-down teacher or clerk who is told that she must have a change of employment, and there are few of us who do not know at least one woman who is a successful farmer. There is a Minnesota woman who owns three hundred and twenty acres of land, and cultivates it herself, hiring help only during harvest. She is considered one of the State's successful farmers, too.

Unless one has sufficient money to buy a farm, one must become a landholder under the Homestead Law. This varies a little in the different States, so it is best to send to Washington for a pamphlet entitled, "Circular from the General Land Office, Showing the Manner of Proceeding to Obtain Title to Public Lands." This contains a great deal of information that will be found useful to the prospective landowner, and should be carefully studied. It contains a list of all the land offices in the different States, and tells what officials should be addressed in the matter of taking up land.

A Dakota writer of experience says:

"One may take a homestead and file on it, which in this State will cost fourteen dollars. She may then take six months before moving on the land. At the expiration of that time she must move to it and live there for about eight months, after which, if she wishes, she may 'prove up' by paying at the rate of one dollar and twenty-five cents per acre and call it her own; or, if she prefers, she may live on the land six months out of each year for five years, and then make what is called a 'final proof,' which is simply calling witness to the fact that she has held her land in good and regular order, and is entitled to a full claim to the same. I think this costs about eight dollars besides the advertising. Any one in the land business can tell you about that.

"The improvements required will be a house or frame dwelling, but that term is quite technical and applies to any board structure, from one six by eight feet in size to the well-built farm house. There must be a well and a certain amount of land under cultivation. Such matters are not inquired into with any very great rigidity, but one must take a solemn oath to the effect that such and such laws have been complied with, and few women would be willing to swear to an untruth.

"When this section of the country was opened up some fourteen years ago many young women took up land. All girls taking up land must be twenty-one years of age in order to do so. Sometimes four frame houses or, in the common parlance, 'shanties,' were located on the adjoining four corners of the four quarter sections forming the whole section of land. This gave them a sense of companionship and neighborliness which was very pleasant. There is something novel, and enjoyable, too, about the free, untrammeled life in the West, where many conventionalities are laid aside and one comes near to nature's heart.

"If desired, final proof need not be made at the end of the five years. It may be delayed until seven years after the first filing, if one wishes to do so. This is a saving in one direction, since taxes need not be paid until the land has come under the 'final proof.' "

Men of experience say that it is often possible to buy land with buildings on for less than the buildings cost, if one watches for such opportunities and stands ready to avail herself of them. So many people start West without due reflection. They delude themselves with the thought that they will become independent quite quickly and pleasantly, and when the reaction comes it is more than they can bear. They can see no break in the cloud that envelops them, and are willing to make any sacrifice in order to get back to their old home. They cannot be talked into seeing the matter in a different light. They are determined to sacrifice themselves, and any one who is fortunate enough to meet them while in this mood will have an opportunity to get a farm for less money than would be required to keep up a claim for the five years designated in the homestead laws.

To go into farming a woman must either be able to do the work herself or she must have some way of earning sufficient money to hire it done for her. She must make the start, fully realizing that, for the first years, there is apt to be more work than money.

All through the East there are abandoned farms which may be had for almost a song. Young men have left them to go into cities or out West, and the old people are no longer able to work them. There are many who are just beginning to realize that money is to be made on these farms, more especially when situated near a good market, and a few years later they will not be bought as cheaply as they may be now. There are many women who are now making money on these abandoned farms. In some respects they are better adapted to work such farms than one in the West, where grain is the principal product.

There is a certain freedom and independence in farm life that, to many, more than compensates for all its hardships. The farmer may be very poor, but it is a different sort of poverty from that felt in the cities, for it brings less degradation.

PAPER FLOWERS.

A little money is to be earned by making paper flowers, if one knows how to do the work artistically. A dainty little old lady in one of our large cities visits the downtown offices, where she finds a market for a great many of hers. In one office there was a large vase of carnation pinks that looked as if they had just been gathered and placed there with artistic carelessness. They were so perfect that they who came into the office stopped to smell of them, and were greatly surprised to discover that they were only paper. They brightened the office for many weeks, and only cost thirty cents.

This old lady never offers a flower for sale until she has learned to make it so well that it is difficult to tell it from the natural blossoms, which she kept before her for a guide. She makes most of her flowers during the summer months, when there is little sale for them, and when she can obtain plenty of natural flowers to serve as models.

When cold weather comes she has many boxes of them neatly labeled and stacked against the walls of her room. Then she watches the social column of the local papers, and when she reads of a prospective entertainment she immediately calls upon those who are to give it to see if they do not want to buy some of her flowers to mix with the natural blossoms in decorating the rooms. They are nearly always glad to get them, for there are many places where they can be used as advantageously as cut flowers, and where the deception is not likely to be discovered. Her heaviest trade comes about the holiday season, and there have been times when she has sold her entire stock and found herself quite unable to supply the demand.

In cities where there are flower festivals and carnivals, or where the windows are decorated at fair time or on any gala occasion, the maker of paper flowers will be sure to find a market for her work. During the holiday season the woman with pretty paper flowers who appears on the scene while a church is being decorated will not be likely to lack a welcome.

BOTTOMING CHAIRS.

A girl whose father had upholstered furniture for a living was left an orphan dependent upon her own resources. She took up such of his work as he had taught her, and which was not too great a tax on her strength, and now she is making a good living recovering worn furniture and putting new cane seats into chairs. She shows considerable business ability, and there is a fair prospect of her being able to reopen her father's old shop before many months have passed away. She will then hire a competent man to do the heaviest of the work.

LACE HANDKERCHIEFS.

Just before the holiday season a young lady may be seen making the rounds of private boarding houses and family hotels. She has dainty handkerchiefs to sell which she has been making ever since the last holiday season. Some are of lace, some hem-stitched, some of drawn work and others of dainty hand embroidery. She sells a handkerchief for a dollar and a half which would cost at least twenty-five cents more in the stores, and she seeks her customers among women whom she knows would be likely to appreciate the real value of her work.

POLISHING HORNS.

One woman, whose home is near a slaughter house in Chicago, makes her pin money by polishing and selling horns. She gets all the horns she can use without paying for them, and does her work so nicely that it finds quite a ready market. Many of them are mounted or made into various fancy articles for the house and office, and others are prepared ready for mounting and either sold as they are or mounted in accordance with the customers' orders.

FANCY BOOK COVERS.

One woman, who knows how to cover books beautifully, makes her pin money by converting her friends' paper-covered volumes into books suitable for the parlor table or library. She uses sateen, denim, art calico, silk — almost any material, in fact, that her employer chances to have and that may be decorated to advantage. One book for a spare bedroom was bound in bed ticking, and made quite a handsome appearance. Often one may buy paper covered volumes in which the print is as good as in the more expensive editions, and these are the ones to select for fancy bindings. Many book lovers are partial to fancy bindings, and this woman sells quite a number of the books she has bound during the holidays and for birthday and wedding presents.

LETTERING.

In small towns and villages, and sometimes in cities, a person with some artistic ability may earn considerable money doing fancy lettering. It is often liked by large dry goods or grocery houses for their shop windows, or by other firms, who thus announce special offers. Mottoes for school rooms and clubs may also be sold, more especially where the worker is able to use colors nicely. At church fairs there is almost sure to be a demand for fancy lettering, where there are fancy booths and a rivalry among the young ladies as to whose shall be most attractive. As a rule, it is best to charge for such work by the hour, and of course one's prices must be low until one has had enough experience to work quickly and to the best advantage.

THE END.